*Critical Guides to Spanish Texts*

C000252938

14  Borges: Ficciones

*Critical Guides to Spanish Texts*

EDITED BY J.E. VAREY, A.D. DEYERMOND AND C. DAVIES

# BORGES

# Ficciones

**D.L. Shaw**

Professor of Spanish
University of Virginia

**Grant & Cutler Ltd**
*in association with Tamesis Books Ltd*

© Grant & Cutler Ltd 1993

ISBN 0 7293 0350 0

*First edition 1976*
*Reprinted with a revised bibliography 1993*

I.S.B.N. 84-599-3302-4

DEPÓSITO LEGAL: V. 214-1993

Printed in Spain by
Artes Gráficas Soler, S.A., Valencia
for
GRANT AND CUTLER LTD
55-57 GREAT MARLBOROUGH STREET, LONDON W1V 2AY

# Contents

*For Mariella*
*in memory of our meeting with JLB*

## Preface

References are to the 1965 edition of Borges' *Obras completas*, Buenos Aires, Emecé, which consists of individual works by Borges bound together irrespective of the dates of the original editions. Thus in what follows:

A is *El Aleph*, 4th edition, 1963
D is *Discusión*, 3rd edition, 1964
F is *Ficciones*, 4th edition, 1965
OI is *Otras inquisiciones*, 2nd edition, 1964
OP is *Obra poética 1923-1964*, 1st edition, 1964

References to the works listed in the Bibliographical Note give the number of the work in italics, followed by the page-numbers, thus: *20*, 143-44.

I have taken the opportunity of this reprint to add some twenty items to the Bibliographical Note. These items, which are numbered *2a*, *2b*, *4a*, etc., are the most important of the many publications on *Ficciones*, and on Borges in general, that have appeared since I wrote this Guide. Some items in the original Bibliographical Note, though once very useful, have probably served their purpose, and I should not have retained them in a rewritten Guide. However, because of references in the text to some of them, I have kept them all. I have revised my comments on some of the other original items.

DLS
March 1992

Borges' early books, from *Fervor de Buenos Aires* (1923) to *Discusión* (1932), his eighth published work, consisted almost entirely of collections of poems or essays. One of the latter, however, *El idioma de los argentinos* (1928), contained what its author modestly called an 'experiment, of dubious value': 'Hombres pelearon'. It was a short narrative piece about a knife-fight between *compadritos* (small-time hoodlums) in a shabby northern suburb of Buenos Aires. Borges wrote in 1970 that it was:

> my first venture into the mythology of the old Northside of Buenos Aires. In it, I was trying to tell a purely Argentine story in an Argentine way. This story is one I have been retelling, with small variations, ever since. It is the tale of the motiveless, or disinterested, duel — of courage for its own sake. (*I*, 73)

Six years later, in 1933, while he was editing the Saturday supplement of a cheap daily paper called *Crítica*, he reworked it into one of his most famous short stories: 'Hombre de la esquina rosada', and the paper published it. It reappeared in his *Historia universal de la infamia* (1935) along with other pieces from *Crítica*. These Borges described as more in the nature of 'sketches' and 'narrative exercises' for popular consumption than real short stories, since they were embroidered versions of actual events, such as the story of the Titchborne Claimant. Thus 'Hombre de la esquina rosada' remained for the moment 'a kind of freak'.

In 1935 Borges approached the short story from a different and more original direction, that of a fake book-review. The idea perhaps grew from an intention to parody the reviews of foreign books he had been publishing in *El Hogar*, a popular illustrated weekly. The result was 'El acercamiento a Almotásim'. It is the first recognizably Borgesian short story, with its characteristic blend of erudition and pseudo-erudition, its playful intellectual humour and serious symbolism, its exotic setting and intriguingly mysterious atmosphere. Like 'Hombre de la esquina rosada', though it occupies a chronologically isolated position in Borges' evolution as a short story writer, it portended the future.  Of it he has written:

> It now seems to me to foreshadow and even to set the pattern
> for those tales that were somehow awaiting me, and upon which
> my reputation as a story teller was to be based.(*I*, 80)

The tales to which Borges alludes really began in 1939.  On
Christmas Eve the previous year he suffered a scalp injury in circum-
stances very similar to those described as producing Dahlmann's
illness in 'El Sur'.  The wound festered and severe septicaemia set in.
For a month Borges was close to death.  On his recovery he deter-
mined to attempt another piece of fake writing, this time a pseudo-
learned article, in order to see whether his creative ability had sur-
vived his illness.  'Pierre Menard, autor del Quijote' proved that it had.
Encouraged. Borges produced in the next two years the six remaining
stories of *El jardín de senderos que se bifurcan* (1942).  They were
written for the most part in the basement or on the flat roof of a
dreary branch-library in a southwestern suburb of Buenos Aires.
There Borges had a miserably paid, but not very exacting, post as a
cataloguer from 1937 to 1946.  'Pierre Menard', and 'Tlön, Uqbar,
Orbis Tertius' which followed it, were published in Argentina's best-
known literary magazine, *Sur*, with which in 1931 Borges had begun
a long and fruitful collaboration.  Ultimately eighteen of his stories
appeared in *Sur* between 1939 and 1952.

Most of the first batch of Borges' tales, then, were written between
early 1939 and late 1941.  By then his production of poetry had
slowed down very perceptibly after the three collections of the 1920s
and been replaced by the rather miscellaneous prose of the 1930s.
To the same period of the early forties belong only a few of the essays
of *Otras inquisiciones* and the first really memorable outcome of
Borges' collaboration with Adolfo Bioy Casares: *Seis problemas para
don Isidro Parodi* (1942).  Borges' relatively slow rate of production,
three or four stories a year at most, underlines the immense care
which he took over them, maturing them in his mind, discussing them
with friends, planning them painstakingly, and finally composing them
phrase by phrase, through numerous successive drafts.  In the end
each is a polished artifact in which every effect is studied and
deliberate.

The arrangement of the stories in *El jardín de senderos que se
bifurcan* follows the order in which they were originally published,

and hence probably written, with the exception that 'Tlön, Uqbar, Orbis Tertius' which begins the collection was, as we have seen, produced after the two stories that follow it: 'El acercamiento a Almotásim' and 'Pierre Menard, autor del Quijote'. Its appearance as the opening story is no doubt due both to its intrinsic importance and to its much greater length. 'La Biblioteca de Babel' and 'El jardín de senderos que se bifurcan' were published for the first time in the collection itself.

In *Artificios* the situation is different. The earliest story to be published was 'La muerte y la brújula' which first appeared in *Sur*, no. 92 (May, 1942), presumably coming too late for inclusion in *El jardín de senderos que se bifurcan* the same year. Next came 'Funes el memorioso' and 'La forma de la espada', both published in *La Nación* in June and July 1942. These were followed by 'El milagro secreto' (1943), 'Tema del traidor y del héroe' (1944) and 'Tres versiones de Judas' (1944). These six stories, together with the eight of *El jardín de senderos que se bifurcan,* constituted the original *Ficciones* (1944). The two stories set in Ireland, 'La forma de la espada' and 'Tema del traidor y del héroe', were evidently set side by side because of this similarity. It is not clear why 'La muerte y la brújula', the longest and one of the most important stories in *Artificios,* does not occupy its natural place at the beginning; but the fact that it does not can hardly be accidental.

Borges' next seventeen stories, written between 1944 and 1952, were collected in the editions of *El Aleph* published in 1949 and 1952. When *Ficciones* assumed its final form in 1956 three more stories had been added: 'La secta del Fénix', 'El Sur' and 'El fin'. They had previously been published in 1952-53 in that order. The alteration of the order, to place 'El Sur' at the end of *Ficciones*, appears to have been dictated by the marked difference between it and the others, and perhaps by the fact that Borges considered it his best short story so far and hence a suitable one with which to round off the book. We must notice, therefore, that the bulk of *Ficciones* belongs to the first half of the 1940s, that marvellously fertile decade in which Borges wrote most of his best-known tales; while the last three items form a separate group added almost eight years later.

The subsequent history of the stories of *Ficciones* emphasizes the preference for the later ones which Borges expressed in the prologue to *Artificios* itself. When in 1951 he published an anthology of his stories under the title of *La muerte y la brújula*, only one, 'El jardín de senderos que se bifurcan',belonged to the first section of *Ficciones*, while the first five of *Artificios* were reproduced. Similarly in *Antología personal* (1961) only 'Las ruinas circulares' appeared from *El jardín de senderos que se bifurcan*, while from *Artificios* Borges chose to reprint 'Funes el memorioso', 'La muerte y la brújula', 'El milagro secreto', 'El fin' and (of course) 'El Sur'. Whether Borges' preference for the second part of *Ficciones* is entirely justified remains a matter of debate.

## II  El jardín de senderos que se bifurcan

### Tlön, Uqbar, Orbis Tertius

'Tlön, Uqbar, Orbis Tertius' is concerned with the deeply-rooted human desire to find in the world some appearance of order and design, and thereby some hope of finality. Borges administers a gentle snub to those who feel this urge, by imagining first a juxta-position and then a combination of two worlds, our own and that of Tlön, in such a way as to suggest certain inescapable conclusions about the former.

One of the difficulties in coming to terms with this story arises from the need to keep separate two rather contradictory aspects of Tlön itself. The first aspect, which every critic has noticed, is that Tlön is the world of pure idealism in the Berkeleyan sense, but going beyond Berkeley in that it involves no need of a God to guarantee the truth and reality of perception. The description of this new world in the second part of the story illustrates what R. S. Mills, in a lucid essay, calls Borges' 'use of the short story of fantasy as a method of exploring the failings of conventional reason' (*32*, 133). The aim here, as Mills discerns it, is to remind us that we do not know what reality is really like. The very acts of perceiving it, and still more of expressing our perceptions of it in terms of language, are selective and arbitrary: a simplification, if not an absurdity. By confronting our instinctively materialist account of the world with an equally congenital idealist one, which seems to be just as coherent or more so, Borges suggests the conclusion that the way we see things is deter-mined not by the things themselves but by our mental categories.

The second aspect of Tlön, which critics including in this case Mills have tended to overlook, is brought into focus by Irby and Dauster. It concerns the fact that the reality of Tlön, though pre-sented by Borges as that of 'un planeta ordenado' with its own 'íntimas leyes', is actually no less chaotic than that of our own world. Its appearance of order is created by the fact that we know it only through a man-made encyclopedia which, like the human mind, imposes an artificial order on the real which it purports to catalogue.

Thus one cannot wholly accept the argument of Weber who, while noticing for example Tlön's 'diversity', 'the unchecked proliferation of metaphysical theories' and 'the immense scope and flexibility of [Tlön's] ideas', seems to over-emphasize its rigorous cohesiveness. Is it really the case that the gradual penetration of our familiar materialist world by Tlön and its idealism would mean the contamination of the latter's rigour by 'the unstable realities of our experienced world'? For, as Weber herself asserts, the 'coherence' of Tlön is 'a contravention of its own principles' (*24*, 128-9). The Orbis Tertius which would result from the insertion of Tlön into our world would not produce ultra-totalitarian order, but redoubled chaos. An indication of this is contained in the fact that the appearance of Tlön inside our world is due merely to a succession of chances. To assume what Weber assumes would be to accept the possibility that a man-made mental construct could ever alter more than the appearance of things. What does emerge from Weber's article is an indirect criticism of Borges' contradictory presentation of Tlön as both chaotic and orderly at the same time. The point to be grasped is that the encyclopedia is orderly and might, like the Bible or Plato's *Dialogues*, influence reality. But its influence would be determined by its contents, which are more chaotic than our chaos. Borges himself does not seem to be completely clear about this distinction. While his presentation of Tlön can be explained at the conceptual level, since Tlön is a kind of parodic mirror-image of our world, it is harder to justify at the aesthetic level. There it tends to confuse the end of the story by leading us to assume that Borges is contrasting Tlön and our world, when it seems more likely that he is rather over-subtly comparing the two.

The opening of the tale illustrates, in a more elaborate way than, say, the beginning of 'El acercamiento a Almotásim', Borges' skill in creating an air of plausibility by deftly mixing together the real and the imaginary. Bioy Casares, Borges' friend and collaborator; Carlos Mastronardi, another friend and fellow writer; Néstor Ibarra, Borges' first translator; Martínez Estrada, the essayist; Alfonso Reyes and Drieu La Rochelle; these are or were all real people. The streets in Ramos Mejía and Buenos Aires are equally recognizable. In this case, of course, the technique itself portends the intrusion of the imaginary into the real which is part of the theme of the story. We must notice, because it supremely affects the interpretation, that this intrusion is from start to finish completely fortuitous. Hence the story begins with a merely chance recollection by Bioy Casares of a passage in an encyclopedia which he had picked up, also by chance. As for the mirror, Rodríguez Monegal, in his essay on Borges' symbols, notes the latter's fear of mirrors in early childhood and almost obsessive mention of them in his work. They are, this critic points out, symbols of the mere outward appearances of things, and of self-inspection. The unreal reflection of the world which they offer suggests the unreality of ourselves as part of it. Here the mirror is placed in conjunction with a fallacious encyclopedia; each reflects something equally unreal: our world and Tlön. Another familiar aspect of 'Tlön, Uqbar, Orbis Tertius' is its use of the detective-story type plot: a mystery at the beginning, a discussion in the middle, a solution at the end.

The first thing we learn about Tlön is the triumph of the gnostics over the orthodox believers, which Mills associates both with the theme of the whole story, 'the arbitrariness of human belief', and with Borges' view that certain beliefs dominate for merely contingent, historical reasons which have nothing to do with their intrinsic content; they prevail, that is, virtually by chance. Chance again, via the person of Ashe, produces the next link in the chain of discovery. Several details here are typical of Borges' manner. Ashe's name, suggestive of greyness, and his fantasmal appearance, prefigure the wizard in the next story Borges wrote, 'Las ruinas circulares'. The book associated with Ashe reveals an unreal world whose apparent coherence undermines confidence in the reality of our own. In a similar way the unreality of the wizard's son compromises his father's reality, and ours. The mention of chess, with its rigid laws and predictability, is made, as in the opening of 'El milagro secreto', to heighten by contrast the chaos of reality here and in Tlön. Finally, Ashe is engaged in transposing mathematical tables, that is, reinterpreting reality.

The description of Tlön which constitutes the third part and the core of the tale is that of 'el planeta que sería la tierra si la doctrina idealista fuera la verdadera descripción de la realidad' (*4*, 50). In Tlön, matter — any concrete object — is held not to exist independently of human perception. It is perception which creates objects, so that reality coincides with the way it is seen. Extreme examples of this are the *hrönir*, at first produced casually, then deliberately and systematically, and the *ur*, which instead of being merely duplicates of previously perceived things, are pure creations of hope. But equally important is the fact that the reality so created consists of 'una serie heterogénea de actos independientes'. The two adjectives, which imply aimless diversity and absence of consecutive causality, emphasize that phenomena in Tlön are no less chaotic than those we are used to.

The languages of Tlön present another important feature. Since in Tlön there are no material objects, there are no nouns; the basic nucleus of language is made up either of verb-tenses (expressing temporal flow, for even in a world of thought time does not stop) or adjectives (which need not necessarily refer to anything which we think of as real, such as the moon, for example, but may like certain Anglo-Saxon *kenningar* have a purely aesthetic purpose). It is just as false, Borges is suggesting, to think that language can express reality, as it is to trust that our perceptions of it are accurate. Thus we are left with thought as the exact equivalent of reality; but thought reduced to a sequence of independent mental perceptions, whose variety can hardly be expressed by language, 'un mecanismo arbitrario de gruñidos y chillidos' (OI, 75). Since the perceptions are 'irreducibles', that is, independent and unrelatable to each other, there can be no systematic thought and hence no science or philosophy. Everything thinkable is as real as everything else. Now Borges is able to mount his favourite hobby-horses one after another: philosophy as mere fantasy, the negation of time, history as cryptography, pantheism, the paradoxes of causality, the modification of what is perceived by the act of perceiving it, the veracity of erroneous literary attributions, the persistence of the physical world only because some living creature is there to perceive it; all these familiar Borgesian notions are knitted together to construct the impression of a world which functions, but whose functioning deprives our world of meaning and purpose.

The '1947 postscript', written of course in 1940 as part of the story, elucidates the mystery of Tlön, revealing it to be the creation of a team of scholars organized and financed by the infidel millionaire Buckley as an act of satanic pride. He and his secret assistants sacrifice themselves in order to create Tlön, whose terms of existence only negate their own all the more. What Borges is telling us is that any attempt to impose order on the universe results in the creation of fiction; it can be no more than a tragic game, futile though heroic. Buckley is the archetype of man, who compulsively imagines schemata and applies them to a world which can contain them, but cannot be contained in them. Deliberately continuing the same paragraph without a break, Borges goes on to something far more striking still: the mysterious appearance of objects from Tlön. As the story began with a symbolic mirror and encyclopedia, so it ends with a symbolic compass and cone. The compass suggests guidance as to the right direction, the cone, aspiration. The human world, longing for a fixed point which the compass seems to indicate, and aspiring to impose a purposive order on the chaos of reality, gladly allows itself to be taken over by Tlön. Borges, meanwhile, knowing that there is no fixed point, and that our aspiration to find out any design in existence is hopeless, goes on indifferently pursuing his own particular brand of literary futility.

Tlön, then, is a transparent metaphor for our world. The encyclopedia symbolizes the coherent mental constructs into which we try to fit it with the aid of language. All man-made explanations of reality are fictitious; but people prefer fictitious design to the recognition that reality is not orderly but bafflingly unpredictable and incomprehensible.

## *El acercamiento a Almotásim*

There is much to connect the first story in *Ficciones* with the second. 'El acercamiento a Almotásim' plainly contains an allegory of existence. The student represents man. India, Barrenechea points out, with its dual associations of the vast and the chaotic, stands for the universe: not for nothing does Borges write in *Discusión* of 'el asiático desorden del mundo' (D, 90). The quest for Almotásim is man's quest for God or for an ultimate explanation of existence. Rejecting the one God of Islam and the many Gods of Hinduism, the student sets off in search of a new absolute. Similar allegories are to be found for example in 'La Biblioteca de Babel' and 'La muerte y la brújula'. The quest begins and ends in the same place,

Bombay, and implicitly leads the student only back to himself. It is, in other words, circular, and to that extent futile. The circular tower from which the quest begins is the first of a host of mocking examples of circularity in Borges' stories. They include the temples in 'Las ruinas circulares', the moon which hangs ironically over Yu Tsun and Lönnrot, the spiral repetitions in 'Tema del traidor y del héroe', and all Borges' labyrinths. At the same time circularity implies that which is all-embracing, as we see from the circular book, God, believed by some to be at the centre of the Library of Babel. This ambiguity is preserved in the student's circular quest better than elsewhere, for we do not know whether the end of the search is positive or negative. One implication could be that by finding only himself the student is baulked, put back to square one. The other, which most critics have accepted, could be that he finally achieves awareness of 'la noción panteísta de que un hombre es los otros, de que un hombre es todos los hombres' (OI, 78) or of the Idealist and Schopenhauerian contention that 'el universo es una proyección de nuestra alma y de que la historia universal está en cada hombre' (OI, 86). The relevance of both these standpoints to Borges' thinking is notorious. But often as he returns to them, in a preface to an anthology of Emerson he has implied that they contain wishful thinking (cf. *9*, 104). Similarly in relation to the quest theme, here and elsewhere in his work, his remark in 1955 quoted by Dauster is of major significance:

> en los libros antiguos, las buscas eran siempre afortunadas; los argonautas conquistaron el Vellocino y Galahad el santo Grial. Ahora, en cambio, agrada misteriosamente el concepto de una busca infinita o de la busca de una cosa que, hallada, tiene consecuencias funestas. (*20*, 145)

Both Dauster and Murillo, who have examined the quest-in-the-labyrinth theme in Borges, strongly emphasize its negative outcome.

To Milleret Borges confessed: 'Je crois que j'ai commencé par des contes hybrides à cause d'une certaine timidité initiale' (*12*, 140).[1] We find evidence of this timidity in his self-restriction to versions of other pre-existing narratives in *Historia universal de la infamia*. But Ronald Christ is right to point out how these 'ejercicios de prosa narrativa' include experiments in narrative method which prefigure

---

[1] I believe I began with hybrid stories because of a certain initial timidity.

Borges' later tales. There is no real break in continuity from, for example, 'El incivil maestro de ceremonias Kotsuké no Suké', through the 'hybrid' or half-way-house stories like 'Almotásim' and 'Pierre Menard' to the more conventionally story-like tales such as 'La muerte y la brújula' or 'El Sur'. Within this evolution, however, 'Almotásim' is the first story in which Borges fully achieved the amalgamation of novel fictional technique and subtle metaphysical meaning which is characteristic of his mature tales. It is, says Ronald Christ, 'the culmination of a sustained effort and the very best of Borges' early experiments' (9, 96).

The basic form of the story is noteworthy in two ways. First, its chief technical originality, the adaptation of a non-fictional form to a fictional purpose, suggests in itself the tenuousness of the distinction between fact and fiction. Second, the design, that of a plot-summary included in a review, seems to reflect the basic theme, Anaxagoras' 'all is in all'. There are four parts, of which the summary is the second and the core of the tale. The opening, that is, the first two paragraphs, once more illustrates the way in which Borges frequently ballasts his completely imaginary creations with allusions to actual people and places. The fantasy is thus subtly engrafted on to the initial impression of verisimilitude; the reader's sense of familiar reality is first deliberately accentuated, then deftly betrayed. Borges never fails to mention gleefully that one of his friends actually tried to order *The Approach to Al-Mu'tasim* from a London bookseller. Guedalla, Watson and Roberts, that is to say nothing of Dorothy Sayers and the Victor Gollancz publishing house, existed as well-known names in the 1930s; reference to them provides the springboard from which Borges launches us off into fantasy.

The plot of the novel itself, which is the essentially fictional part of the tale, is, we notice, vaguely related to the detective story; hence the reference in the opening to its 'mecanismo policial'. The appeal to Borges of these stories, with their combination of crime, coldly intellectual analysis and the suggestion of the universal quest for truth, was very great and, as we shall see, inspired one of his finest productions, 'La muerte y la brújula'. The *'undercurrent místico'*, on the other hand, refers to what really distinguishes Borges' best stories, the fact that they 'develop ultimately from metaphysical notions' (9, 101). We also recognize the theme of the world seen as

a vast book when in his account of the last nineteen chapters of the
novel Borges refers to the vast dimensions of its setting and to the
all-embracing way it expresses the complex movements of the human
spirit. In this respect Mir Bahadur Alí's novel is entirely at one with
Ts'ui Pên's in 'El jardín de senderos que se bifurcan'. M. D'Lugo, in
one of the relatively few articles which analyze Borges' fictional
technique rather than his meaning, demonstrates how the non-
fictional frame of the story (the pseudo-review), with its investigation
of variants and discussion of sources, functions in parallel with the
exposition of the novel's plot which is also an investigation. The
frame and the content, that is, are complementary and operate on
the reader in concert, both to manipulate his credulity and to reinforce the idea of a hidden epistemological problem.

As a rule every major detail in a typical Borges story can be
assumed to have been deliberately introduced and to have a specific
function in relation either to the story's structure or to its meaning.
Examples are the chess game at the beginning of 'El milagro secreto'
or Recabarren's paralysis in 'El fin'. Thus no story by Borges can
be regarded as fully interpreted until each detail fits. An illustration
here is the iron stair by which the student climbs to the round top of
the tower (cf. Lönnrot in 'La muerte y la brújula' who 'subió por
escaleras polvorientas a antecámaras circulares'). Several flights of
the iron stair are missing; we are not told how the student reached
the top. Since the tower is symbolic (it is, we notice, both circular
and connected with death), the stair is almost certainly symbolic too.
It seems to prefigure the mystical quest on which the student is about
to embark. The quest begins with a rational decision: the student
'piensa', 'arguye' and at length 'resuelve'. Thereafter this 'libre-
pensador' prays! Reason has led to faith and faith to the mystical
quest for God. But the missing flights in the staircase which led the
student to his point of departure seem to suggest that this apparently
consistent upward progression involves movements between levels —
the rational, the spiritual and the mystical — which are not in fact
connected to one another.

Some discrimination is of course required in regard to such details.
A.C. Pérez sees the wall which the student climbs over as separating
his exterior life from his inner life, and the dogs as the fallacies of
religious belief. His interpretation of the meaning of the tower, the

well, the corpses, the gold teeth and other elements in the description, coming on top of the rest, begins to seem far-fetched (*14*, 138).

The third part of the story, which corresponds in this mock-review to the critical discussion and evaluation of the novel, can be seen as allusive to Borges' own ideas about how his stories should be read. We notice that he distinguishes between the 'variada invención de rasgos proféticos' (or what amounts broadly to the main aspect of the plot) and the symbolism of the work. So long as the former predominates over the latter Borges is content to praise Bahadur's 'buena conducta literaria'. When in a later edition 'la novela decae en alegoría', and meaning (i.e. unambiguous meaning) outweighs inventive originality, Borges is critical.. Here we have a plain statement of his priorities. It is less misleading than his constant protests against looking for meaning in his work, for these protests are contradicted by many of his own most illuminating statements. The second distinction which we find in the paragraph is between those details which imply an anthropomorphic monotheism and the concept of a God who is himself in search of a God. This distinction not only underlines Borges' rejection of the traditional Christian conception of the divinity but also introduces the idea of a double circularity into the story. The student's quest, which is circular and implicitly futile, is for a God who in turn is 'un peregrino' engaged on a similar quest. As in 'Las ruinas circulares' we are caught up in an infinite regression.

The end of the tale introduces the poem of the Simurg. Further references to it in 'Nota sobre Walt Whitman' and 'El enigma de Edward Fitzgerald' in *Otras inquisiciones* show how much it struck Borges' imagination. It rounds off the story by symbolizing poetically the student's discovery, which was already hinted at by the reference to mirrors in the sub-title of the second edition of Bahadur's novel: there is no ultimate outside the self; the microcosm includes the universe.

## Pierre Menard, autor del Quijote

Both 'Las ruinas circulares' and 'Pierre Menard, autor del Quijote' are basically concerned with the mind's urge to transcend its own limitations, combined with the idea of bringing into being a new element of reality. One branch of human activity above all seems to be connected with this double desire: artistic creation. So much is this the case that Ronald Christ sees 'Pierre Menard' as 'an allegory for what the artist does' (*29*, 64-70). Each new work of art or literature is an addition to reality, akin to a living entity, which interacts with its surroundings through the minds on which it exerts an influence. Borges has repeatedly asserted, apropos of Shakespeare and Coleridge in particular, the degree to which a writer's works transcend his own personality. It is therefore ironic that literary creation should figure prominently in Borges' work in connection with the theme of the impossible task. This is doubly so in the case of 'Pierre Menard' since Borges has stated that after writing it 'I saw that I could go back to literature and . . . feel that my life was in some way justified' (*10*, 54).

As commonly with Borges' stories, it is useful to distinguish between what 'Pierre Menard' is intrinsically about, and what its implications are. Borges begins from the premiss that all language implies a past series of events which has created the present-day associations and meanings of words by a deterministic causal process. Similarly, each individual human being includes in himself the entire past that has produced him. So Borges writes in 'La escritura del Dios':

> decir *el tigre* es decir los tigres que lo engendraron, los ciervos y tortugas que devoró, el pasto de que se alimentaron los ciervos, la tierra que fue madre del pasto, el cielo que dio luz a la tierra . . . toda palabra enunciaría esa infinita concatenación de los hechos. (A, 118)

Menard himself is therefore the product of a past which is three centuries longer than that which produced Cervantes, a past which is therefore infinitely richer and more variegated. Similarly the words and ideas of *Don Quixote* itself have been enriched since the book's first publication by a host of new associations. To write *Don Quixote* in 1939, even using the same words, is consequently to write a quite different book. Hence Borges' remark to Burgin apropos of 'Pierre Menard': 'that story has the idea . . . that every time a book is read or re-read, then something happens to the book' (7, 22). Since no two readings are identical, no two writings of the same book are identical; if only because time has modified the associations of the words. Three centuries having intervened 'cargados de complejísimos hechos', 'el fragmentario Quijote de Menard es más sutil que el de Cervantes'. D. Newton de Molina in a lively essay takes this to be one of Borges' deliberate misstatements of his own views and praises the story's irony accordingly (*34*). Because of Borges' remarks to Burgin, I am dubious, but with Borges one can never be certain.

Commenting on the technique of the story, Borges described it as being, like 'Almotásim', 'still a halfway house between the essay and the true tale' (*1*, 84). As the former was a bogus book-review, so this is a bogus semi-necrological article or memoir, once more adapting a non-fictional technique to a fictional subject. In form it consists of two descriptive sections contrasting the 'visible' publications of Menard with his 'invisible' re-creation of part of *Don Quixote*, followed by the somewhat fulsome assessment of his achievement which is usual in such writings. A feature of the opening compilation of pretended publications, the idea for which (and for all his other bibliographical jokes) Borges took from Carlyle, is the close connection of some of them with Borges' own work and interests. For instance, b) is not unrelated to Borges' early poetic manifestos; c), d) and h) reflect his close interest in specific aspects of philosophy (cf. his essay 'El idioma analítico de John Wilkins' in *Otras inquisiciones*); while k) illustrates his fascination, for a time, with Quevedo. Behind Menard we are quite deliberately intended to see Borges. In the same way, but less importantly, the initial B of Bachelier, Bacourt and Bagnoregio points in each case directly to the author. Menard's 'casi divina modestia', and his habit of affirming the reverse of what he actually believed, link him closer still to his creator. We cannot overlook this connection when we see that Borges judges Menard's task to be 'una empresa complejísima y de antemano fútil' and that he remarked much later to Charbonnier 'Il y a chez lui un sens de l'inutilité de la littérature (*8*, 161).[2] Barrenechea is right to suggest that 'Pierre Menard' expresses a 'vision of the writer as non-creative' (*5*, 46). Borges, that is, does not exclude literary endeavour (including his own) from his scepticism about the value of all human endeavour. Hence his habit of presenting his stories as 'games' played with metaphysical concepts, and the writer's work as revealing in the end only 'the shape of his own face', that is, the configuration of his own

---

[2] There is in him [i.e. Menard] a sense of the uselessness of literature.

personality and nothing more. It is noteworthy also that one of Menard's speculations concerns the creation of 'objetos ideales' to satisfy purely poetic necessities. This and the identity of all personalities (e.g. Menard's and Cervantes') prefigure very obviously 'Tlön, Uqbar, Orbis Tertius', the next story Borges was to write. Menard's *Don Quixote* is in fact a kind of *hrön.*

The second section of the story is the most striking and audacious part, very effectively introduced via the brusque contrast with the catalogue of nineteen items which precedes it. For the most part it playfully describes the aim, method and difficulties of Menard in re-writing *Don Quixote.* But it contains two elements of particular significance. One is Menard's statement apropos of his task: 'Me bastaría ser inmortal para llevarla a cabo.' In 'Funes el memorioso' Borges writes: 'tal vez todos sabemos profundamente que somos inmortales y que tarde o temprano, todo hombre hará todas las cosas.' We are not far, that is, from Borges' hypothesis that an infinite time-sequence means in the end the repetition of every previous event. But if Menard's task is related to the concept of circular time on one side, on the other it has to do with the equally Borgesian theme of order, chaos and causality. The reference which Menard makes, albeit obliquely, to 'el término final de una demostración teológica o metafísica' is not insignificant. For Menard to succeed in his task would be to prove that the world and causality exist objectively in such a way that certain chains of determinism (e.g. those which produced Cervantes and thus in turn *Don Quixote*) can be deliberately re-created. At the same time it would prove that time can be made to become circular. The obvious impossibility of fulfilling such aims augments the folly and grandeur of Menard's attempt.

The last section, which begins with the assertion that Menard's *Don Quixote* surpasses Cervantes', rests on the contrast between a reading of the text with modern associations and a reading of it by seventeenth-century eyes. Every event modifies every other event by its intervention in the chain of causality. How then can we, whose world-view has been altered in the interval by the absorption into contemporary thought of the ideas, for instance, of Nietzsche and William James, read Don Quixote's Speech on Arms and Letters or Cervantes' views on history in the sense in which they were originally written? We notice too that while Cervantes was contrasting the 'real' of his own day with the imaginary world of romance, Menard is contrasting two equally unreal dimensions of life: his own twentieth-century awareness of the 'real' of Cervantes' time and the world of chivalry. Literature, Borges is once again suggesting, can never tell us anything about the ultimately real, or about life, except that they are unknowable. Here Borges and Menard join hands again finally. For if what has just been said is true, Borges' own work can also be viewed as 'una empresa complejísima y de antemano fútil'. Both 'Pierre Menard' and 'Almotásim' announce the impossible task as Borges' basic theme.

## Las ruinas circulares

In a number of lectures and interviews Borges has referred to 'Las ruinas circulares' as occupying a unique place in his memory. Barrenechea quotes from an interview given in 1960 the statement that ' . . . the tale was carrying me along. But this has occurred only once' (5, 149). Borges went on to amplify the remark as follows:

> When I wrote 'The Circular Ruins' I was employed in a local library. It took me eight or nine days to write this story and I remember that during that period I would leave my house, take the trolley to the library, work, return to my house, and all that seemed unreal; what seemed real, instead, was the tale I was dreaming, the story I was living at that time. I also recall that I had no difficulty in writing it . . . everything came to me as if it had been established already, as if it had been dreamed previously by another person. This is the story I wrote with the greatest ease. That is, I had the feeling of future generations which might interest themselves in it. (5, 151)

One of the clues to the story's meaning is the often-quoted passage from the end of 'Magias parciales del *Quijote*' in *Otras inquisiciones.* The theme of this essay is that of interior duplication in works of imagination: the play within a play, the story within a story. '¿Por qué nos inquieta que el mapa esté incluído en el mapa y las mil y una noches en el libro de *Las mil y una noches*? ', Borges asks. He goes on: 'Creo haber dado con la causa: tales inversiones sugieren que si los caracteres de una ficción pueden ser lectores o espectadores, nosotros, sus lectores o espectadores, podemos ser ficticios.' What Borges does in 'Las ruinas circulares' is to identify the reduplication

directly with existence itself through the relationship between creator
and created. The inspiration for the tale, he told Richard Burgin, was
the phrase from *Alice through the Looking Glass* quoted beneath the
title: 'And if he left off dreaming about you . . . '

Readers of Unamuno's *Niebla* will recognize a familiar theme, that
of life as a dream: reality is an illusion; we exist in the mind of God
in the same way that merely fictional characters exist in the minds
of writers. The idea has a long history in both eastern and western
thought; only the expression of it in Borges is new. In his version,
however, the emphasis should not be overlooked. While Calderón in
*La vida es sueño* and Unamuno in his novel both postulate, with
different degrees of conviction, a true reality (the divine mind)
behind the illusion which we call the real, Borges leaves no such
doorway open. Already in a poem he had asked:

> ¿Qué dios detrás de Dios la trama empieza
> De polvo, y tiempo y sueño y agonías?   (OP, 182)

There is no First Cause, only an infinite regression into which everything meaningful ultimately dissolves.

Two features of the opening of the story reveal this emphasis.
The key-word of the title is *circulares*. It is re-echoed in the description of the temple in the first paragraph as a 'recinto circular' and a
'redondel'. Circularity, already prominent as we have seen in Borges'
first mature story 'Almotásim', thus reappears as a symbol both of
endless futility and of universal oneness. In the same paragraph
circularity reappears in a temporal guise when the temple is described
as already having been devoured by ancient forest fires, a fate which
recurs at the story's end. We notice too that these circular temples
seem to occur successively along the banks of a river which, as A. C.
Pérez suggests (*14*, 90), possibly symbolizes human history. The
idea of futile repetition in time is therefore again emphasized.
Secondly, Irby and Alazraki have drawn attention to the first adjective
in the opening: 'unánime'. The night is 'single-souled' in the sense
that it exists in the mind of a single individual: the other wizard who
is dreaming the one described.

The setting of the story in the East is explained by Borges' statement: 'As for the Orient, although it exists as a reality, it has also
existed since the time of Marco Polo and since the Bible entered into
man's imagination, as a type of dream. The Orient is now the

embodiment of unreality' (5, 149). It is therefore the appropriate backcloth for a story in which, as Borges stresses in the prologue to *El jardín de senderos que se bifurcan*, 'todo es irreal'. One of the principal technical features of 'Las ruinas circulares' is the fact that, unlike other stories in *Ficciones*, it contains no element of familiar reality to shore up the fantasy. Three features of the presentation of the wizard prepare the reader for the rest of the story. The first is physical: his wounds, which he did not feel, heal at once. We suspect them to have been unreal. Our suspicion is confirmed by the wizard's immunity to fire at the end of the story. The second is mental: the wizard sleeps by an act of will. This portends his future ability to control matter by force of volition as he controls his own bodily activities. Once more we accept the idea only by deliberate suspension of disbelief. Thirdly we notice that the climactic sentence of the opening paragraph, marked by the slightly incantatory repetition: 'sabía que ... sabía que ... sabía que ...' converts his 'invencible propósito' (his subjective choice) into an 'obligación' (dictated by someone else).

The announcement of the theme, which follows in the second paragraph, draws our attention afresh to the impossible task as a general theme in Borges' stories. Finding Almotásim, finding a 'libro total' in the Library of Babel, re-writing *Don Quixote*, finishing a play in front of the firing-squad: all these attest Borges' deep involvement with the mind's desire to transcend its own limitations. The wizard's task in this case is closely linked to that of Buckley in 'Tlön, Uqbar, Orbis Tertius'. It is that of creating by a combination of will and imagination a new element of reality capable of existing on equal terms with those already in being. The impossibility of the project warns us to regard the story as a kind of allegory and to examine primarily its implications. As in the case of 'Tlön' what we perceive is that an artificial, imaginary entity seems to acquire an autonomous substantial existence. When it is revealed to be false, its source and origin is revealed to be false also.

Unamuno had argued that a fictional figure may be more real and alive than a human being. In *Niebla* a threat to the existence of one becomes a threat to the existence of the other. Borges' idea of a deliberate, organized and systematic dream is another way of expressing the parallel between life and fictional creation, for creative writing closely resembles conscious, disciplined dreaming. But the metaphor is reinforced by the suppression of any direct allusion to fiction as such: the wizard's creation is presented as real in a way that Unamuno's Augusto Pérez is not. What in *Niebla* is the mere similarity of author and character, becomes in Borges' tale the relationship of father and son.

The technique of the story is governed by the need to bring about the accomplishment of the wizard's task slowly, through successive stages, to a climax near the end of the story when the illusion is brusquely shattered. After the announcement of the theme in the second paragraph we discern three distinct phases in the wizard's activity. The first is one of failure. The wizard attempts to operate by selection and elimination: his dream here suggests vaguely the dream of reason. The method, predictably, proves uncreative. The second phase is one of partial success. Inverting his procedure, the wizard abandons the general, the external and the abstract. He turns to the internal and the concrete: the heart of the individual. At once his dream, perhaps the dream of the emotions, becomes more creative. But the creature he dreams remains stubbornly asleep. The third phase, in which he evokes supernatural aid like the student in 'Almotásim', is one of apparent success. In his third dream, in a sense the dream of the spirit, his new creation awakes.

Hitherto the creature of the wizard's dream has been referred to variously by indeterminate designations ('alumno', 'mancebo') or by deliberately dehumanized expressions ('su obra', 'el fantasma soñado'). Now he becomes 'mi hijo': he has achieved parity with human existence. This is the centre of balance of the story: creation has been accomplished, reality has been attained. Now Borges begins to develop the counter-process. Already certain indications have been inserted to prepare it. The boy's features 'repeat' those of the wizard; the latter is worried by his impression 'de que ya todo eso había acontecido'; most of all, Borges intervenes to warn the reader that the wizard would have done better to destroy his creation. Ronald Christ suggests that the test by means of which the 'son' proves his autonomy by planting a flag on a distant hilltop (i.e. by modifying external reality) contains a further clue through Borges' use of the verb 'flameaba' (*26*, 10). Alazraki sees yet another in the reference to the '*mil y una* noches secretas' employed in the son's creation. The *First Encyclopedia of Tlön*, we recall, had 1001 pages (*4*, 55). The number in both cases is meant to put us on our guard.

The culmination of these indications is the news that the wizard's son is now famous for his ability to tread on fire without being burned. This is symbolic of his non-existence as a real human being. All that remains is to reapply it to the wizard himself. When the forest fire reaches the temple, the wizard's fears for his son prove applicable to himself. The end of all his labours is the realization that he too is insubstantial, a mere figment of imagination, that any sense of his own ultimate reality (Unamuno's *alma de bulto*) is a mere illusion.

The wizard's reaction is not unlike that of Tzinacán in 'La escritura del Dios' (*El Aleph*) or Borges' on perceiving the total universe in 'El Aleph'. Dauster remarks: '[It] may be the resignation of understanding: it may also be the resignation of total horror [at] an experience which reveals the fundamental truths of existence, and which awakens a feeling of resignation and a willingness to accept death, possibly because the alternative, once perceived, is too horrible to accept' (*20*, 143-4). The fire-God who is referred to in the story is simply a device, probably suggested by Heraclitus' belief in fire as the origin of all things. A God of fire, that is to say an ultimately destructive divine principle, is sufficiently self-contradictory not to conflict with the meaning of the story.

The tale's structure, in which reality is laboriously created only to be revealed as unreal, and the form of the wizard's creative process, which proceeds from chaos through selection to purposeful integration, only to be shown as pointless, leave us with the feeling that 'Las ruinas circulares' is a parable of scepticism.

## La lotería en Babilonia

If there is no design in the universe, all is fortuitous; if the world is chaos, chance reigns supreme. 'El argentino', Borges once asserted, 'siente que el universo no es otra cosa que una manifestación del azar' (OI, 220). He himself, more cautiously, wrote in a poem of

> El vago azar o las precisas leyes
> que rigen este sueño, el universo. (OP, 203)

In one of Herbert Quain's books, *The God of the Labyrinth*, the

meeting between the chess-players, apparently casual, in fact appears
to illustrate symbolically the 'precise laws' of a determinism which,
whether or not we recognize it, may perhaps rule our lives. In 'La
lotería en Babilonia', Borges suggests the other possibility. We perceive here the relevance of G. Bickel's emphasis on Borges' dualism,
or as another critic calls it: 'that tension between a desired harmony
and a witnessed destruction which characterizes the vision of his
work'.[3] The basic symbol of this story, the lottery itself, illustrates
this dualism. For a lottery is an organized event and differs from the
ordinary workings of chance by that very fact. The relation between
chance and the lottery in this tale is the same relation that exists
between chaos and the labyrinth in Borges' general outlook. That is
to say: just as the labyrinth appears to have a meaningful design
leading to the centre, but in Borges' conception is most probably
purposeless and circular, with no centre to be reached and no exit
save death, so the lottery appears to be a meaningful organization
of chance by the mysterious 'Company', but is probably in reality
no more than the blind disorder governing our lives. Both symbols,
the labyrinth and the lottery (like the library in 'La Biblioteca de
Babel'), combine an appearance of design with an implied reality of
futile chaos.

The attraction of this combination lies not only in the fact that it
reflects exactly the way Borges thinks things actually are; it lies also
in the fact that this combination reflects the configuration of our
own minds (including, of course, Borges' mind). We suspect that
life is an aimless maze, but we cannot avoid seeking significance in
those elements discernible in it which appear to suggest a pattern; we
feel deep down that all is chance, but we cling instinctively to the
hope that all chance is really unseen direction. Hence one of the
important features of this story is the fact that the people of Babylonia
clearly prefer to believe in the existence of the 'Company' and to
view the lottery as 'una interpolación del azar en el orden del mundo',
than to follow the heresiarchs who, as in Tlön, indicate the direction
which Borges himself is pointing to in the story. It is of course
always possible to see, along with N. D. Isaacs and Dauster, Art as the
specific manifestation which the inherent human desire for order

[3] A.L. Weinstein, *Vision and Response in Modern Fiction* (Ithaca, N.Y., 1974),
224.

takes on in the case of a creative writer like Borges. In other words, we may also interpret the elements of design which are characteristic of the labyrinth, the lottery and the library, as symbolic simply of literary form, of intellectual constructions imposed specifically by Art on the chaos of existence. Thus the relevant stories could be at once broadly about life and man's instinctive desire to reduce it to some interpretation, religious, philosophical or whatever, and narrowly about life and the writer's instinctive desire to reproduce it in terms of a literary form. The point in both instances is that 'a *meaningless* system of order is the weapon against the despair-producing formlessness of life' (*43*, 387, italics mine). Hence Borges' futile, but orderly, activity – translating *Urn Burial* in Quevedan language, not for publication – at the end of 'Tlön, Uqbar, Orbis Tertius'.

'La lotería en Babilonia' is then, as its opening informs us, about something which is 'parte principal de la realidad', but which can be seen in two ways. There is the consecrated, conventional way of viewing it, preferred by the majority; and there is a 'blasphemous', heretical way of viewing it, restricted to an unorthodox minority. The narrator who supplies this information is the most interesting of all Borges' narrators in *Ficciones*. These fall into four loosely differentiated classes: the omniscient narrators of 'Las ruinas circulares', 'La muerte y la brújula' and various other stories, including in a sub-category the not quite omniscient narrator of 'Tema del traidor y del héroe'; the scholar/reviewer/critic of 'El acercamiento a Almotásim', 'Pierre Menard', etc.; the rather more unbuttoned pseudo-autobiographical Borges of 'Funes el memorioso' and 'Tlön, Uqbar, Orbis Tertius'; and finally the class of first-person narrators other than Borges, that is, those who are actually involved in the stories they tell, such as Moon, Yu Tsun, the librarian of 'La Biblioteca de Babel' and the Babylonian. Undoubtedly the last two narrators are the most intriguing, since Borges makes no attempt to present them realistically in any way, or to explain to whom they might conceivably be telling their stories. Paradoxically it is they above all who come nearest to representing mankind generally, since in each case they are consciously at grips with a world they do not understand.

But there is a major difference. The librarian is inside the library. The Babylonian, for an unspecified reason, is outside Babylonia, and able to view its customs with a degree of detachment. The former is a seeker; the latter is a commentator. The narrative rôle is different, and the difference illustrates afresh the extreme care and precision with which Borges constructs his stories, down to minimal details. The fact that the Babylonian narrator is about to take ship and leave his interlocutor cannot be without significance; nor can the fact that he lacks his right index finger. Either he is about to re-enter the world he has briefly left (so that distance has lent perspective), or the ship is Charon's vessel and the narrator is about to leave life itself for ever (so that the moment before death has brought with it its traditional insight). The lack of the finger which normally serves to point things out or indicate direction symbolizes concretely the incertitude, the subjection to aimless circumstance, which is referred to more directly later in the opening paragraph and is the theme of the story as a whole. The Babylonian is archetypal man, as the first sentence of the tale suggests, caught in a characteristically circular existential pattern: Beth on moonlit nights dominates Ghimel but is subordinate to Aleph, which on moonless nights is subordinate to Ghimel. Now he is suddenly granted the ability to contemplate, for a moment, his destiny.

The method Borges adopts in the story is to take the familiar lottery whose tickets were in fact, as in the story, sold by barbers in Argentina, and develop it along lines suggested by the evolution of organized religion. Ultimately it becomes synonymous with the human condition (everyone is compelled to take part, everyone is subject to its rules). Positive explanations of how it works become synonymous with religious interpretations of man's experience; negative explanations (those of the heresiarchs) become synonymous with non-religious, non-purposive interpretations. The main structural feature of the first part of the story is offered by the successive stages in the process by which the lottery is transformed into an image of reality. There are four such stages. In the first, monetary forfeits are introduced alongside prizes. In the second these are extended to include prison sentences; as a result prizes and forfeits cease to be purely financial and come to include all forms of happiness and sorrow. In the third stage the lottery becomes free, secret, universal and, of course, compulsory. Finally chance is allowed to invade even the workings of the lottery itself. It has now become identical with life in all its bewildering multiplicity of possibilities.

But already, in the middle of a paragraph (as usual), Borges has almost imperceptibly shifted the emphasis. By the time that even the organization of the lottery comes to depend on chance, with all that this implies about the organizer, the reader's interest has begun to be deliberately diverted towards the underlying question of the existence and operation of the 'Company' (God) supposedly running the lottery. The fact that the final stage in the evolution of the lottery itself is separated from the first three by this shift of emphasis is technically highly significant. By postponing it in this way Borges is able to interpolate it into his discussion of the 'Company' and by this means not only to lock the two halves of the story firmly together, but also to use the final stage of the lottery's evolution to reinforce the implication that the 'Company' is non-existent. This implication seems to dispose of A. C. Pérez's view that the 'Company' symbolizes the State and not God, a view which makes nonsense of the story's meaning. Isaacs mentions the importance of the reference to 'masked' heresiarchs at the end of the story and to the appearance of the 'Company's' ambiguous 'pieza doctrinal' amid the debris of a mask-factory. In both cases what is implied is that the utterances, though disguised as false, are true. Both utterances suggest that all is pure, directionless chance. We notice without surprise that the laws of the lottery are described as labyrinthine, and that the sacred place of the Babylonian God is a labyrinth. Life is a maze; if a God is responsible for it, his purposes are totally indecipherable.

The end of the story depicts a world in which on the one hand, as Borges wrote in a similar context, 'toda estrafalaria cosa es posible' (D, 102), while on the other hand certain scholars (read: theologians, and historians who profess to discern a pattern in history) pretend to have a reliable method of reducing this existential chaos into some kind of order. Their disagreements Borges ironically attributes to wilful deceit of the public, and not to error. The last dozen or so lines, the climax of the story, accumulate alternative hypotheses to the traditional religious one symbolized in the myth of the 'Company'. Presented as 'abominable', 'heretical' and 'vile' in conformity with Borges' playful habit of deliberately misleading his less alert readers, these alternative hypotheses, following rapidly on one another, complete the pattern of the latter part of the tale. It is that of gradually developing the idea that the operations of the 'Company' are unpredictable and absurd and its existence a contradiction of experience. The last two hypotheses (that the 'Company' does not, and never will, exist, and that all is mere interplay of chance) in fact assert the same thing: there is no God and no discernible order in the scheme of things. Traditional belief that the opposite is the case is simply part of the 'queridas costumbres' of our 'Babylonian' world.

## *Examen de la obra de Herbert Quain*

Of the stories in *Ficciones* this is one of those which have received least critical attention, which perhaps implies that it is one of Borges' less successful tales. It belongs, with 'Pierre Menard', 'El jardín de senderos que se bifurcan' and 'El milagro secreto', to the group of stories which in one way or another explore the mutually ambiguous relationships which Borges seems to postulate as existing between literature and reality. In this case, though we perceive the similarity of approach in this and the other two stories, the effect of ambiguous parallelism seems to be less satisfactorily achieved. Borges appears to be too identified with Quain. In the works mentioned in the story we are struck as usual by the 'invención', the imaginative originality, to which Quain attaches such importance; but we do not recognize behind it the level of meaning which we normally expect of his creator Borges.

Quain's four books have this in common with the novels of Mir Bahadur Alí and Ts'ui Pên, and with Hladík's play, that they can be seen as involving familiar Borgesian attitudes towards the real. *The God of the Labyrinth*, is, like the future 'La muerte y la brújula', a detective-story with a difference. We can assume it to be a kind of metaphor. The 'enigma' is both the problem facing the detective and the enigma of life. Behind the apparently convincing and generally accepted solution to it lies another more 'real' solution. In other words, behind those interpretations of existence in rational and orderly terms, which render it comfortably comprehensible in broad outline while at the same time making allowance for chance (i.e. freedom), there perhaps lies a different interpretation based on an iron law of determinism whose workings can only be glimpsed when apparently casual events turn out to have been crucial.

*April March* reminds one of the novels in Tlön which 'abarcan un solo argumento con todas las permutaciones imaginables'. If we assume some degree of causal sequence connecting the chapters to one another, the structure of the book suggests the idea of predictability seen in reverse, with a Final Cause (z) to which $x^{1-9}$ are in some way connected via $y^{1-3}$: the apparently contradictory order of events appears to have been resolved retrospectively into some sort of order. Men would prefer an even simpler scheme, but the Gods choose an infinite interlacing with no First Cause, no predictability, no possibility of unravelling the labyrinthine interconnected sequences of causality. *The Secret Mirror* is clearly adapted from the same previously existing dramatic idea which Borges was to use more effectively in 'El milagro secreto' (see below p. 61). Here too an attractive conventional pattern of events (those of Act One) is revealed to be a mere imaginary reflection of a much less agreeable one. Our picture of existence, that is, might bear the same artificial relationship to existence as it really is, that the scenes of Act One in *The Secret Mirror* bear to those of Act Two.

All three of Quain's works, then, are wilfully ambiguous. They seem to express the ambiguity which exists between what we assume, or pretend to ourselves, that reality is like, and Borges' vision of an unpredictable, bewilderingly contradictory and almost certainly purposeless scheme of things. But whereas in other stories Borges uses his characteristic Chinese-box-like principle of construction with subtly significant interior duplication, here the three story-outlines are merely juxtaposed. Borges remains satisfied with a simple effect of re-emphasis. This might have been no less effective than his other constructional principle if it had been possible to see a climactic element in the sequence of Quain's three works. It is possible to argue, certainly, that *April March* implies a more nihilistic vision of life than *The God of the Labyrinth* (in which an element of design, albeit hidden, subsists), while *The Secret Mirror* goes even further than *April March* by suggesting the unreliability of the mental mechanisms themselves by means of which we reach our picture of the real. In this way a sort of progression can be read into the order in which the three story-outlines appear. But it is less than wholly convincing. Equally, while the playful tone of the introduction and the conclusion, with their obvious references to Borges' own fictional manner, are probably designed to give a deliberately frivolous false impression of the significance of Quain's work, and hence alert the happy few to its inner meaningfulness, we cannot be wholly sure. It may be that Borges, the 'amateur protestant' as he once called himself, is here only protesting against the culpable futility of Art, which travesties God's creation by trying to express it in human terms.

The ending is a verbal pirouette. Quain's last work, *Statements*, contains eight stories, like the 1942 edition of *El jardin de senderos que se bifurcan*. In the same way, each of the stories is deliberately ambiguous. From the third of Quain's stories Borges alleges that he took the fourth of his (in 1941) future collection, which is here announced ('Herbert Quain' appeared first in *Sur* in April 1941). Borges, that is, supposedly took a story from a book he himself had imagined and included it in a forthcoming book of his own, modelled on the former. All, as usual, is one and the same. With familiar symbolic circularity Borges imitates a story written by a character in one of his own stories: the real and the fantastic meet and fuse.

## La Biblioteca de Babel

Speaking to Georges Charbonnier in 1965 Borges said:

> Dans 'La Bibliothèque de Babel' je dirai qu'il y a deux idées. Il y a d'abord une idée qui n'est pas mienne, qui est un lieu commun, l'idée d'une possibilité de variation presque infinie en partant d'un nombre limité d'éléments. Derrière cette idée abstraite, il y a aussi (sans doute sans que je m'en trouble beaucoup) l'idée d'être perdu dans l'univers, de ne pas le comprendre, l'envie de trouver une solution précise, le sentiment d'ignorer la vraie solution. Dans ce conte, et je l'espère dans tous mes contes, il y a une partie intellectuelle et une autre partie — plus importante je pense — le sentiment de la solitude, de l'angoisse, de l'inutilité, du caractère mistérieux de l'univers, du temps, ce qui est plus important: de nous mêmes, je dirai: de moi-même. (*8*, 20) [4]

---

[4] In 'The Library of Babel' I should say that there were two ideas. There is first of all an idea which isn't mine, which is a commonplace, the idea of a possibility of almost infinite variation beginning with a limited number of elements. Behind this abstract idea there is also (no doubt without my letting it bother me much) the idea of being lost in the universe, of not understanding it, the desire to find a precise solution, the feeling of not knowing the true solution. In this story, and I hope in all my stories, there is an intellectual part and another part — more important, I think — the feeling of loneliness,

Two words indicate the basic theme of this story, which Borges in 1970 called 'my Kafkian story' (*1*, 84). They are the word 'mundo' which replaces 'biblioteca' in the last paragraph and the word 'Babel' in the title which (cf. the possibly related English 'babble') implies chaos or confusion. The opening paragraph describes a library partly modelled on the one in Almagro Sur where Borges was working when he wrote it. The number of shelves and the number of books on each were simply borrowed from reality and have no significance. The rigid geometrical pattern of each section of the library, endlessly repeated, suggests order and the idea that a single intelligence had created the infinite structure according to a coherent and recognizable plan. The oblique reference thus made to the argument for God's existence sometimes known as 'the argument from design' is both obvious and deliberate. But when the contents of the bookshelves are examined, the exactly opposite impression emerges: all is unintelligible chaos. This is, as the first two words in the tale tell us, Borges' vision of the universe: chaos with the teasing semblance of order. The librarians (mankind, particularly thinking men) are obsessed with the desire to resolve the contradiction between the appearance of the world, seemingly created according to design, and the evidence which more and more in modern times seems to deny the existence of a designer. They are seeking a key to the labyrinth; but, as Isaacs observes, 'the only way out is over the banister into the abyss' (*43*, 387).

The choice of the metaphor is explained in two earlier essays by Borges: 'La biblioteca total' (*Sur*, no. 59, August 1939, 13-16) and 'Del culto de los libros' (*Otras inquisiciones*) which refer to the idea of existence as the book of God. The essence of Borges' treatment of the metaphor in this story is its surprisingly unambiguous negativity. The entire tale reads simply like an explanation of Borges' affirmation in *Otras inquisiciones:*

> cabe sospechar que no hay universo en el sentido orgánico, unificador, que tiene esa ambiciosa palabra. Si lo hay, falta conjeturar su propósito; falta conjeturar las palabras, las definiciones, las etimologías, las sinonimias, del secreto diccionario de Dios. (OI, 143)

of anguish, of futility, of the mystery of the universe, of time, what is more important still: of ourselves, I should say: of myself.

These words: definitions, etymologies etc., which are not only unknowable, but, it seems, even beyond conjecture, are the contents of
the library's books.

After the opening descriptive paragraph, in which the presence of
the mirror reproducing the appearances of appearances already portends the futility of any quest for an ultimate reality behind them,
the story is largely dominated by this very quest. But instead of presenting it dramatically, Borges uses a technique approximating to
that of an essay, just as he had done in 'El acercamiento a Almotásim'
(cf. *9*, 99) and elsewhere. The basic structure of the tale, that is, can
be seen to fall into three parts: first, the initial description, the first
statement of the problem, the reactions of the Idealists and Mystics,
and the promise of a solution; second, the development of the problem, axiomatic assertions, the history of the quest for a solution
(i.e. a First Cause), the rôle of the 'inquisitors', contrasting extreme
reactions, arguments and refutations; third, a pseudo-solution. Just
as the imaginary novel in 'Almotásim' supplies the story's fictional
element, so here the appearance of a story-line is supplied simply by
having a first-person narrator, but as in 'Tlön, Uqbar, Orbis Tertius',
'Pierre Menard', 'Tres versiones de Judas' and elsewhere, we look in
vain for plot.

The particular form which the Borgesian theme of the impossible
task takes in this story is the quest for an explanation of existence:
'el catálogo de catálogos', 'un libro que sea la cifra y el compendio
perfecto de todos los demás', 'un libro total'. The fact that men
have always sought it; the fact that the library (the universe) shows
signs of design, predictability and repetition; the fact that there is no
case of 'un solo disparate absoluto' (i.e. a failure of cause and effect);
the need for a First Cause: 'El origen de la biblioteca y el tiempo'; the
assumption that somewhere amid the infinite variety of reality lies
the key to its pattern; all these conspire to perpetuate the quest.
But when we come down from the world of abstractions and broad
philosophical principles to the world of everyday concrete experience
(the chaotic letters of the individual books) the semblance of order
dissolves. The letters are recognizable and repetitive, but their order
is meaningless. Attempts to interpret them produce only the comic
contradictions satirized in the reference to 'un dialecto samoyedo-
lituano del guaraní, con inflexiones de árabe clásico'. Only one

reading is clear: 'Oh tiempo tus pirámides'. A pyramid symbolizes man's triumph over time, since those of Gizeh are among man's oldest and least destructible monuments. Pyramids of time symbolize time's triumph over all things: one of Borges' most haunting intuitions.

The activities of the various inhabitants of the library symbolize the variety of human reactions to the problem of finding an explanation of existence, and to the difficulties of the quest. The mystics assert a central room visible only to the eye of ecstasy; the idealists partially elude the problem by relating the design of the library to what the human mind is intrinsically capable of perceiving; certain inhabitants become professional investigators: philosophers or theologians, 'inquisitors'; fanatics struggle, dispute and destroy; others despair. A detail which links the story with 'La lotería en Babilonia' is the way in which some of the library's inhabitants, overcome by the futile regularity of their surroundings, resort to shuffling discs in a dicebox (i.e. to gambling, like the Babylonians) in order to find relief in imitating 'el divino desorden'. Despite Borges' attempt to maintain a balance by referring to those who despair as 'impíos' and by insisting that 'es verosímil que esos graves misterios puedan explicarse en palabras' which must exist somewhere, it is clear that these concessions to man's hunger for the absolute are ironic. Borges is himself an 'impío' in this sense, and an inhabitant of the 'región cerril' of the sceptics.

Hence the 'solution' proposed in the last paragraph is only a pseudo-solution: a deliberate paradox. What is unlimited cannot be periodic (i.e. recurrent). At best one can have recurrence within limitlessness — the Nietzschean idea of Eternal Return which we find underlying 'Tema del traidor y del héroe'. So, either the 'solution' is self-contradictory, or, because circular (like the library/universe itself, which the story describes as 'una esfera'), futile.

## El jardín de senderos que se bifurcan

Also to Charbonnier Borges remarked apropos of 'El jardín de senderos que se bifurcan':

> Je crois que deux idées sont à l'origine: l'idée du labyrinthe, qui m'a toujours hanté, et du monde comme labyrinthe, et aussi une idée qui n'était qu'une idée de roman policier, l'idée d'un homme qui tue un inconnu pour se signaler à l'attention

d'autrui ... Je crois que ce qui est plus important que l'histoire policière, c'est l'idée, c'est la présence du labyrinthe, et puis l'idée d'un labyrinthe perdu. Je me suis amusé a l'idée non pas de se perdre dans un labyrinthe, mais dans un labyrinthe qui se perd aussi lui-même. (*8*, 131-2) [5]

Like 'La muerte y la brújula', that is, 'El jardín . . .' combines suspense and adventure with metaphysical implications in a manner developed from Stevenson and Chesterton. In both stories the adventure aspect provides an apparent 'solution' (the devices employed by Scharlach and Yu Tsun), but the real problem implicit in them is of an existential kind and has no solution. The ease with which the practical issue is resolved (by violence) mocks our impotence in the face of the abstract, existential problem: the universal quest for some understanding of life. One cannot unravel life's meaning, Borges suggests. Only those puzzles which are the result of human contrivances can be resolved; life's contrivances are too bafflingly labyrinthine.

The spy-story, then, exists as a frame for the story-within-a-story: the account of the meeting between Yu Tsun and Stephen Albert. In itself this spy-story is sufficiently novel and ingenious, though much less elaborate than the detective-story element in 'La muerte y la brújula'. Himelblau in his article on 'El jardín . . .' points out both that the reference to Liddell Hart is deliberately inaccurate (a typical Borgesian joke) and that historically speaking Yu Tsun's action would have been perfectly futile, since the Germans were well aware of British activity around Albert. This last point is more important than it may seem. One of the critical problems connected with 'El jardín . . .' concerns the relation between the frame-story and the rest. Once we see Yu Tsun's action as pointless and Yu Tsun himself reduced to the level of 'un títere envuelto en esfuerzos inútiles' (*36*, 39) leading ironically, like Lönnrot's, to his own death, the problem disappears. Another significant detail is that Yu Tsun is a character borrowed from the novel *Hung Lu Meng* (by Tsao

---

[5] I think that two ideas are behind its origin: the idea of the labyrinth, which has always haunted me, and of the world as a labyrinth, and also an idea which was just a detective-story idea, the idea of a man who kills a stranger to attract someone else's attention to himself . . . I believe that what is more important than the detective story is the idea, the presence, of the labyrinth, and after that of a lost labyrinth. I amused myself with the idea, not of losing oneself in a labyrinth, but in a labyrinth which also loses itself.

Hsue-Kin, 1791) mentioned in the text. The fact re-emphasizes his unreality as an active human being.

The structure of the tale is tripartite. The first part, which ends with the reference to the moon accompanying Yu Tsun, establishes the spy-story frame. Borges, when introducing Yu Tsun's *declaración*, predictably imitates Lönnrot: brushing aside Liddell Hart's common-sense explanation of the delay to the allied offensive, he proposes instead the more intellectually satisfying theory of Yu Tsun's intervention. It is, however, no less false (as we have just seen) than Lönnrot's theory of the Hassidim. The rest of the frame, still like the opening of 'La muerte y la brújula', illustrates afresh Borges' superb ability to excite the reader's curiosity and suspense, in this case by the threat of death established in the second paragraph followed by Yu Tsun's mysterious reference later to 'la única persona capaz de transmitir la noticia'. It also exemplifies his method of including what he called 'worked-in' or 'inlaid' details, which recur like call-signs in his work. These include Yu Tsun's reflection: 'Siglos de siglos y sólo en el presente ocurren los hechos', prefiguring the symbol of the cat in 'El Sur'; the reference to Goethe, reflecting the familiar Borgesian idea that to repeat an action or a thought is to become momentarily one with its originator; the reference to the mirror (always a sinister, threatening presence in Borges) in which Yu Tsun takes leave of himself, an unreal entity ironically bidding farewell to a shadow; and finally the reference to the 'circular' moon, like that seen by Lönnrot, which points forward to the circular gramophone record turning beside the bronze phoenix and to the 'vívido círculo de la lámpara'. These circularities not only suggest the futility of Yu Tsun's eventual gesture, but also, as Ronald Christ observes, symbolize the idea of 'cyclical time hinting at the reincarnation of Ts'ui Pên in the form of Albert' (*9*, 124). They also bring to mind the idea of the labyrinth, which in Borges is always to be thought of as circular. Chance, which gives Yu Tsun forty minutes' start on Madden and brings him via a telephone directory into contact with Albert, again plays a characteristic rôle in this story.

The second part of 'El jardín . . . ' opens with a reference to labyrinths. Two features above all of the labyrinth commend it to Borges as a symbol of existence or reality. The first derives from the fact that labyrinths are man-made, and, though bafflingly chaotic, have an appearance of regularity and order. The same notion is visible in the order, containing chaos, of the Library of Babel. Borges seems to suspect that, though a mysterious causal pattern may govern existence, man's attempts to impose such a pattern on life and reality merely lead him into a self-created labyrinth. The second feature of labyrinths is the idea that they suggest a search for a hidden centre. Man's search for ultimate truth, for God, for an explanation of life, is a quest for the centre of the existential labyrinth. In contrast to Rodríguez Monegal I believe that for Borges each man is the centre of his own labyrinth; his quest, like that of the student in 'El acercamiento a Almotásim', is circular and leads back to himself, or to death.

The interview between Yu Tsun and Albert falls into two parts divided by the latter's reading from Ts'ui Pên's book. The first part explains the riddle of the lost labyrinth. Ts'ui Pên's novel and his famous labyrinth are not separate entities, but one and the same thing. Here a difficulty arises. We know that the book is equivalent to the labyrinth and the labyrinth to life. But the description does not fit. The book is worse than chaotic, it is contradictory. The second part of the interview explains the difficulty by developing Albert's mysterious earlier remark that the book contains 'un invisible laberinto de tiempo'. When we think of existence as baffling, we think of a chaos of events which resist our attempts to organize them into a meaningful causal pattern. It is this chaos that Borges had alluded to in 'La lotería en Babilonia'. Here he goes a stage further. However chaotic the events of life may seem, we nevertheless think of them instinctively as occurring in chronological sequence. What Borges now suggests is that the notion of chronological time may be something which we artificially (and falsely) impose on events, just as we artificially and falsely impose meaningfulness on them. Existence may be composed of a multiplicity of time-sequences: 'una red creciente y vertiginosa de tiempos divergentes, convergentes y paralelos', of which we habitually perceive only one strand. A hint of the same multiplicity, as G. Bickel points out, is visible in the structure of the story itself at this point. Yu Tsun's narrative contains the novel of Ts'ui Pên, and is therefore chronologically later; but Ts'ui Pên's novel also contains the story of Yu Tsun.

The specific alternative to the notion of straightforward chrono-logical time which chiefly interests Borges is, of course, circular time, the idea of eternal recurrence. This concept underlies Yu Tsun's reaction to the last words of Albert's reading from Ts'ui Pên. The events of the novel seem to Yu Tsun to prefigure the events in which he himself is involved; like the heroes of Ts'ui Pên, he also is resigned to killing and dying. The fiction of Ts'ui Pên momentarily incor-porates the 'reality' of Yu Tsun's situation. Once more, at the end, Yu Tsun, before killing Albert, enjoys a brief vision (like that of Borges in 'El Aleph') in which the other dimensions of time seem to appear to him.

In reply to Irby's question of why Yu Tsun carried out his plan to murder Albert, despite his discovery of all that they had in common, Borges declared:

> Yu Tsun doit tuer Albert pour que l'effet soit bouleversant, pathétique. La personne qu'il tue doit compter pour lui; autrement, cela n'aurait aucun sens. Il est plus pathétique que Yu Tsun tue un homme ayant su comprendre l'énigme de son propre ancêtre, un homme devenant presque son parent. De plus, comme Albert est une espèce de Dieu, un homme extra-ordinaire, peu importe qu'on le tue, ne trouvez-vous pas? Voyez-vous l'ironie? Albert a déchiffré une espèce de cripto-gramme en comprenant le sens de l'oeuvre de Ts'ui Pên, et, à son tour, lui-même — c'est à dire son nom — fait partie d'un autre cryptogramme. (25, 394) [6]

L. A. Murillo suggests that Albert's discovery is flawed by the omission of one detail. Unlike Yu Tsun, he seems not to know that Ts'ui Pên had originally been murdered by a foreigner (13, 167). If this is the case, it adds irony to Albert's situation. The rest of Murillo's commentary, which analyzes the story in terms of free will and determinism, is sharply criticized by A. C. Pérez who sees it as a misinterpretation of Borges' intention. A technical feature which we

---

[6] Yu Tsun must kill Albert so that the effect may be upsetting, pathetic. The person he kills must mean something to him; otherwise it would be quite senseless. It is more pathetic that Yu Tsun should kill a man who has managed to understand the enigma of the former's own ancestor, a man who has almost become one of his relations. Moreover, since Albert is a kind of God, an extraordinary man, it matters little that he should be killed, don't you find? Do you see the irony? Albert has deciphered a sort of cryptogram by understanding the meaning of Ts'ui Pên's work, and in turn, he himself — his name, that is — becomes part of another cryptogram.

notice is that the gradual discovery of Ts'ui Pên's novel and its contents is in a way related to, or carries with it, Yu Tsun's growing reverence for Albert, whom he must kill, and attachment to him. This reinforces the pathos Borges himself alludes to.

Finally the guillotine, cunningly hauled up in the second paragraph of the story, is allowed to fall. Madden arrives and Yu Tsun's vision is dissipated. But Yu Tsun's arrest and condemnation, and even his apparently successful signal, are reduced, by what he has learned of life from the talk with Albert, to the level of the unreal and the insignificant. The realization that his action in killing Albert is linked to 'innumerables futuros' (hence the latter's 'immortal' face) renders his contrition 'innumerable'.

## III Artificios

### Funes el memorioso

Borges' description of 'Funes el memorioso' as 'una larga metáfora del insomnio' requires a brief explanation. Before writing the story Borges had been suffering from insomnia for about a year. What struck him about the experience was the inescapable lucidity of sleeplessness in contrast to the total forgetfulness of sleep. Hence the remark at the end of the story that 'dormir es distraerse del mundo'. The contrast was heightened, he explained in a lecture at Brown University in 1967, by the fact that in Argentine Spanish *recordar* and *recordarse* are sometimes used for *despertar* and *despertarse*. Funes' memory, that is, represents compulsory, total lucidity, ineluctable awareness of every thing whatsoever that falls within his area of perception. At first sight it is a metaphor of universal insight and knowledge, one of mankind's oldest dreams. But, as we know from 'Tlön, Uqbar, Orbis Tertius', there can be no such knowledge. In 'Tlön' Borges had made the point that our perception of reality is in itself arbitrary: merely 'one way' of seeing things. In 'Funes' he develops the further point that our perception is arbitrary partly at least because it is selective. Funes can remember, in the subtlest detail, every thing he has ever seen; but he cannot think. For to think is to choose, to separate out (forgetting the rest) certain elements of perception and to organize them into a conceptual scheme or pattern which is then reapplied to reality. As Borges explains:

> La simplificación conceptual de estados complejos es muchas veces una operación instantánea. El hecho mismo de percibir, de atender, es de orden selectivo: toda atención, toda fijación de nuestra conciencia, comporta una deliberada omisión de lo no interesante . . . nuestro vivir es una serie de adaptaciones, vale decir, una educación del olvido. (D, 69-70)

Funes' accident has destroyed this faculty of adaptation in him and at the same time ironically provided him with an unlimited store of the raw material of perception. He becomes, in Borges' own words, 'simply a gigantic memory and as such incapable of intelligence' (*29*, 447). 'Funes', clearly, is a less fundamentally negative story than

'Tlön'. From the latter we learn that we may not be able to see reality as it actually is; from 'Funes' we learn that this is a blessing. Funes sees reality as pure flux, indeterminate and chaotic. He is over-whelmed by circumstance, drowned in futile details; while, fortunate-ly for us, 'nuestra mente es porosa para el olvido' (A, 169).

In essence the story is a fable: that of the man who achieves what men long for, only to find that the magic gift brings misery instead of happiness. In this case, however, the lesson is an intellectual, not a moral, one. The construction of it is relatively simple. After the opening paragraph, 'Funes' consists of four clearly defined parts. The first two are introductions to the third: the interview with Funes in 1887, which is the kernel of the tale. It is followed by a group of closing reflections and the stark reference to Funes' death. There is no plot, drama or suspense. Once more, as in 'Pierre Menard' and 'Almotásim', Borges simulates a non-fictional form for the story. It is presented as a memoir designed to form part of a symposium of similar accounts: 'el volumen que editarán ustedes'. Technically this is simply a device for obtaining an immediate effect of credibility, but in the general context of Borges' work it can also be seen as another expression in formal terms of his readiness to identify fact with fantasy. The use of the first person narrator performs its normal function of shortening the distance between the reader and the events narrated, but here it is used much more prominently than in, say, 'Pierre Menard' to supply the framework of familiar reality into which the figure of Funes is inserted. Of all the stories in *Ficciones* this is the one in which Borges as narrator, interlocutor and commen-tator has the most developed rôle. The reason is clear. Unlike Menard or Quain, Funes is not an intellectual; he cannot be presented in-directly through his writings. He has no thoughts and is physically immobilized; he cannot be presented through his ideas or actions. The only solution is a direct encounter. It is most convincingly told in the first person. Intrinsically Funes is hardly more than a personi-fication of memory. The fact that he seems so much more alive than the student in 'Almotásim', for instance, is due to the first-person technique. Funes draws his reality from Borges the narrator.

The reiterated 'recuerdo' of the initial paragraph does more than announce the theme. It underlines (in retrospect) the contrast be-tween Borges and Funes, and serves as a further element knitting the form of the tale and its content indissolubly together. For this story, which is about memory, is a selection of Borges' memories organized as a narrative. Borges shows by the very act of telling the story that he — and we — can do what Funes could not do. Borges, that is, can extract elements from the remembered reality of fifty years earlier and express them as a rational construct. The opening paragraph ends with three brief remarks, the last of which is distinctly contemptuous in tone; their function is to suggest the narrator's detachment and objectivity.

The main technical problem which Borges must now have faced in writing the story was that of gradually inducing the reader to accept Funes' amazing uniqueness. How does he do it? The time notation at the beginning of the second paragraph, together with the circumstantial and visual details which follow, are designed to create a vivid impression of concrete reality focusing rapidly on Funes and culminating deliberately in a further repetition of the key-word 'recuerdo'. At this point Borges (having prepared his effect) shifts without warning into the slightly fantastic. Funes, this commonplace rural *compadrito*, can tell the time precisely without a watch and can remember without effort all the baptismal names of a mere acquaintance. The incident establishes him momentarily as no more than an interesting freak with a reputation for *rarezas* in his home town. But it plays its part in the mechanism of the story by leading the reader toward the much greater suspension of disbelief which the interview with Funes will require. This in turn is separated from the meeting just mentioned by a much longer passage of pseudo-real details, closely connected with the narrator, into which Borges carefully introduces a graduated sequence of elements connecting the Funes of 1884 with the Funes of 1887: his fall from his horse; his unexpected satisfaction with his state of paralysis; his letter, with its precise recollection of the three-year-old date and extraordinary request; finally, his recitation of the chapter on memory from Pliny in the original Latin. Partially disguised by the apparent shift of interest away from Funes and back towards the narrator, his studies and his father's illness, these elements continue the process of converting the original reference to *rarezas* into Funes' fantastic gift of memory.

The crucial interview, therefore, does not have to bear all the

weight of transmitting the realization of Funes' extraordinary endowment to the reader; it only completes the process which is already
under way. The reference to Pliny acts as a hinge on which the story
turns smoothly into the totally fantastic, carrying the reader with it.
This ability to carry off a smooth transition, often in the course of
the same paragraph, from one order of narrative events to the other is
the source of some of Borges' most successful effects. With a deft
reference back to the first mention of Funes' surprising powers
Borges connects them as they were before the accident to their
amazing development after it. Then they were striking; now they
are infallible. At the same time we perceive the significance of Funes'
earlier ability to remember details and to tell the time exactly without
a watch. His new-found ability is also dual: *percepción* and *memoria*.
Not only can Funes perceive the present in all its chaotic multiplicity
as easily as we can see three glasses on a table; he can also recall
every instant of his own conscious past just as totally. His vision is
complete. A feature of the paragraph which describes Funes' double
capacity is, however, its prominent irony. The passage begins and
ends symmetrically with illustrations contrasting Funes' awareness of
reality with ours, apparently to our disadvantage. But in his italicized
remarks we recognize a carefully graduated anti-climax. This is
developed in the later reference to Funes' system of numbers and its
'disparatado principio'. Barrenechea remarks: 'the comic strain in
names and motivations or the foolish catalogue of his memories
appease any enthusiasm over his angelic intuition of the world.
[They] degrade the concentrated vision of the planet, making it
absurdly comical' (*5*, 84). The same function is performed by the
deliberate stylistic contrast Borges builds up by juxtaposing references
to the 'teeming' and 'urgent' reality of Babylon, London and New
York with a reference to Funes' 'pobre arrabal sudamericano'. These
incongruities emphasize the point that Borges is making. Funes'
mind, in Wheelock's phrase, is 'primordial chaos', his endowment 'a
fatal ineptitude' (*15*, 29). Symbolically, Funes dies of *congestion*
of the lungs.

'Funes el memorioso' illustrates superbly one of the things which
make Borges seem unique as a short-story writer: the intellectual
quality of his creativeness. Even when we compare him with
Unamuno at his most abstract (in, for example, 'La historia de Don

Sandalio, jugador de ajedrez') or with Pirandello or Kafka, the exclusively mental inspiration and carefully designed conceptual framework of his most typical short stories is what strikes the reader most. Where we find a similar combination of fantasy with an equally tightly organized frame of reference appealing deliberately to the mind is in certain forms of satire: in Quevedo or Swift. What Borges does essentially is to apply the procedures of this kind of satire to a deeper level of human error and folly than that which normally occupies satirists: to man's conception of reality.

Putting it another way: in 'Nathaniel Hawthorne' (*Otras inquisiciones*) Borges distinguishes between authors who think in images and those who think in abstractions. When the latter attempt the rôle of the former the result is usually pleonastic and frigid. But Borges himself is obviously an exception. The abstract and the imaginative are inseparably and successfully fused in his prose work. Neither deforms the other.

## *La forma de la espada; Tema del traidor y del héroe; Tres versiones de Judas*

These three stories can be thought of as forming a single sub-group in *Ficciones* unified by the themes of treachery and guilt. Since these themes recur prominently in other stories and poems by Borges we may presume that they have a strong private significance for him, just as they had for Joseph Conrad. On a less personal plane we may relate the theme of treachery to that of ambiguity of personality and thereby to those works of twentieth-century literature which imply the loss of our old sense of possessing a single personal identity. Stevenson's *Dr Jekyll and Mr Hyde* is of course the most famous early example.

Borges told Burgin that 'La forma de la espada' was 'one of the stories I like least, because it's a trick story after all' (7, 131). The trick, naturally, is the ending, in which the reader discovers that the narrator of the infamous treachery of Moon is none other than Moon himself. His aim, Borges explained, had been to let Moon stand outside his own story, and at the same time to increase the pathos of Moon's subsequent remorse by suggesting that it compelled him to tell his story with no attenuations or excuses. The device produces a most effective and unlooked-for climax to the story. It would otherwise have been difficult to bring it to a suitable end without introducing a new element to indicate some form of punishment for Moon's crime. As it is, the compulsion behind the narration-confession, driving Moon to lay bare his own abjection, is the penalty he suffers. A question which arises is whether the last sixteen lines or so (i.e. after 'No me duele tanto su menosprecio . . . ') are really effective or necessary. The infliction of the wound, which refers back immediately to the opening sentence of the story, and the unexpected allusions by the narrator to his story as 'esa confesión' and to his hearer's contempt, are surely adequate in themselves to suggest that Moon is telling his own story. The following lines merely make the suggestion completely explicit for the benefit of less attentive readers.

The real critical question posed by the story, however, concerns not the effectiveness or otherwise of the trick ending, but Moon's reflections in the paragraph beginning: 'Entonces comprendí que su cobardía era irreparable' (F, 133). For here Borges attempts, a little clumsily, to insert the suggestion that the particular narrative method adopted in this case is not just a novel technical device intrinsic to the story itself, but is related to the idea that 'cualquier hombre es todos los hombres'. Moon is not just assuming his victim's rôle, but is in some way the victim himself. If this were so, the effect of the narrative method would be to place 'La forma de la espada' in a category similar to that of 'La muerte y la brújula' considered as a metaphor of suicide. Once more the distinction between betrayer and betrayed would become blurred and the reader would be left uneasily aware that similar antitheses co-exist within his own personality. It is questionable, however, whether the notion that the victim might have felt momentarily contaminated by Moon's cowardice, supported by the reflections which follow the enunciation of this notion, are in fact wholly sufficient to confer a deeper meaning on this ingenious, but slight, tale.

The case of 'Tema del traidor y del héroe' is rather different. Robert Scholes, in his brief commentary on it, emphasizes the deliberately non-realistic opening, with its pointed allusions from the first word of the title onwards to the fact that we are reading something essentially fictional. But what is the function of such an opening in the general mechanism of the tale? It is to throw down a frank challenge to the reader to dismiss the story as a mere fantasy, to scorn any attempt to see in it a serious comment on reality. The reader who is familiar with Borges' habit of saying, or implying, the opposite of what we are intended to conclude, is instantly alerted.

The Chestertonian element in the story is, as in 'La muerte y la brújula', the construction of an apparently weird and mysterious concatenation of events, which later turns out to have been the contrivance of some single individual. The reference to Leibniz in the next line is more ironic. It is connected with the fact that the intricately harmonious order of events described in the story is not (as Leibniz suggested with regard to reality) a naturally harmonious disposition of things, but an artificial creation of the imagination, borrowed — more ironically still — from the enemy country's national poet. Once more design, order, meaningful recurrence, are merely constructs of the intellect or of Art. What is interesting in this case is that the imaginative construct subsequently affects actual events, not merely by conditioning Ryan's response a century later, but in the meantime by prefiguring the death of Lincoln. As in 'Tlön, Uqbar, Orbis Tertius' the imaginary invades the real.

The pattern of 'Tema del traidor y del héroe' is the familiar one of a quest or search for the solution to a mystery. When found, as in 'La muerte y la brújula' or 'El acercamiento a Almotásim', the solution seems to involve certain philosophical issues. Ryan, Scholes notes, discovers himself to be playing a part in a fictional work designed by Nolan. His rôle moreover, like Nolan's, is that of a falsifier of history. Time and events once again follow a circular path. History is once again seen as cyclic when the death of Caesar is vaguely reflected in those of Kilpatrick and Lincoln. A noteworthy feature in this connection is the fact that Kilpatrick's death, like Lincoln's but unlike Caesar's, occurs in a theatre. What Borges prefers to envisage is an infinite circularity of time which, like the infinite circularity of the Library of Babel, suggests both eternity and futility. But in common with Azorín (though for a different reason) he chooses to imagine slight differences or discrepancies between one cycle and another. For, as the end of 'La Biblioteca de Babel' suggests, a perfect correspondence between one cycle and the next would imply order and possibly purpose. This Borges wishes to minimize, though we can hardly escape the conclusion that any theory of cyclic time suggests some kind of order. Ts'ui Pên's theory of proliferating time-scales is more in accord with Borges' vision of all-embracing chaos on which the mind or the artistic imagination strives to impose patterns.

The similarity in the deaths of Caesar, Kilpatrick and Lincoln alludes to the Borgesian idea that one man is all men, that every person and event contains everything that has gone before. Nor is this all. For the relationship between the real Kilpatrick and the historical figure created by Nolan is the relationship between the traitor and the hero. In this case their identity one with the other is more successfully emphasized than in 'La forma de la espada', for the two Kilpatricks, the hero and the traitor, are in this case actually one and the same man. The distinction is not merely blurred by a cunning narrative device; it does not exist at all. Finally we recognize again here the symbolic Chinese-box effect of some of Borges' stories which was first noticed with regard to 'Las ruinas circulares'. Ryan exists as a character in the work of Nolan. But Nolan is a character in a work by the 'Borges' who is planning to write the story 'en las tardes inútiles'. In turn this 'Borges', together with his useless afternoons, is a persona of Borges himself who, as he wrote in a poem, suffers from:

esta agonía
de ser enigma, azar, criptografía.          (OP, 159)

A typically regressive sequence dissolves finally into complete mystery.

Carried to its final conclusion, the idea that hero and traitor may be one and the same, suggested in 'La forma de la espada' and more successfully developed in 'Tema del traidor y del héroe', leads in 'Tres versiones de Judas' to the identification of Christ, the ultimate hero, with Judas, the archetypal traitor. Christ would thus become a suicide. During his stay in Geneva in the early 1920s, Borges tells us in 'Una vindicación del falso Basílides' (*Discusión*), he became interested in the gnostic heresies of the early Christian era. They undoubtedly strengthened his 'afición incrédula y persistente por las dificultades teológicas' (D, 9). This taste for the more esoteric forms of theological speculation led him eventually to Donne's *Biathanatos* and to Phillip Maïnlander, an obscure (possibly apochryphal) latter-day gnostic who, Borges says, killed himself in 1876. The idea of such a figure, a modern Basilides, probably suggested that of Runeberg. The latter is, of course, simply a device to express the intriguing paradox on which the tale is based.

The form of the story is again that of a pseudo-article in a learned magazine briefly passing in review the work and ideas of Runeberg. In line with the pattern already established in 'El acercamiento a Almotásim', the narrator adopts for the most part an impersonal, scholarly tone, presenting imaginary details as facts and, as usual, juxtaposing references to real people (De Quincey, Almafuerte, Euclydes da Cunha) with others to non-existent writers (Abramowicz, Erfjord and – drolly enough – Hladík, whose imaginary book is cited by an imaginary theologian to confute an imaginary objection). Once more the form adopted alludes artfully to the content, the unity of opposites: fiction is presented deliberately as non-fiction.

After a brief introduction stressing the affinity of Runeberg's beliefs and those of the gnostics as well as the passionate sincerity with which his beliefs were held, Borges divides his exposition of these last into three stages. As always in his fictional work, the method aims at a prepared effect. The strategy of the story is to move by careful steps from one level of paradox to a second and finally to a third. This last is the climax, the ultimate paradox, for which the preceding stages will have prepared the way. In the first Judas accepts an almost unthinkably tragic destiny. Recognizing the need to balance Christ's divine sacrifice with a corresponding human one, he voluntarily condemns himself to eternal infamy and to hell. In the second stage, though his action is the same, his motive is different. As lesser ascetics mortify the flesh, so he now imposes on himself the supreme mortification of the spirit. As others renounce earthly joys, so he renounces, in a spirit of 'gigantic humility', eternal salvation, gladly accepting endless obloquy and punishment in the knowledge that Christ is happy in Paradise. These two stages combine to suggest to the reader superhuman qualities of sacrifice and renunciation in Judas. In the third stage this suggestion of a superhuman capacity for suffering is replaced by a straight identification of Judas with Christ. Christ redeems mankind by descending, not merely to human form, but to the lowest depths of man's spiritual degradation. Only thus is the sacrifice perfect.

So far the story has the impersonal unity of tone and the careful

organization of argument of the 'article' it purports to be. It builds
up to its object of inducing us to entertain momentarily the dizzy
hypothesis that Christ might have been Judas, that the most remote
of opposites might have been one and the same, that our fundamental
assumptions — even in the realm of faith — might be too arbitrary.
As in 'Tlön, Uqbar, Orbis Tertius' Borges indirectly induces us to
question our concept of the real, so here he extends the process to
involve our conception of the divine. The very least that can be ˈsaid
of the story so far is that it contains some remarkably probing satire
of Christian concepts. But at this point the tone changes. The last
three paragraphs no longer contain detached reporting of Runeberg's
arguments. The manner changes abruptly from that of an article to
that of a short story with an omniscient narrator. Runeberg no
longer 'sugiere', 'observa', 'prosigue', 'arguye'; the verbs now are
'intuyó', 'comprendió', 'sintió', and 'recordó'. Borges is no longer
pretending to rehearse evidence, he is making direct authorial statements about his character's inner experience. As in 'La forma de la
espada', it is a question of bringing the story, which has no plot
as such, to a satisfying end. Borges' decision is to conclude the tale
with a reference to the traditional punishment for those who approach
the divine too closely: madness. The decision compels him to alter
the tone from the expository to the genuinely narrative. The climax
is logical and effective, but it is achieved at the expense of the story's
unity of technique.


## La muerte y la brújula

To James Irby Borges said: 'I wrote "Death and the Compass"
following Chesterton a bit. It is possible that in adding that detail of
the straight line, I was thinking of his story called "The Horsemen of
the Apocalypse" ' (quoted in 9, 115). The mark of Chesterton does
in fact seem particularly strong on this story. One recalls particularly
'The Man who was Thursday' whose labyrinthine plot in the end
turns out to have been the work of Sunday. Borges has always
evinced a very strong interest in detective stories and at one time
directed the publication of a famous series in Argentina (El Séptimo
Círculo) which brought out about 150 of them. He also wrote such
stories in collaboration with Bioy Casares. Borges has explained his

interest in detective stories as being due to their very meticulously constructed plots ('in a detective novel everything is very nicely worked in' (7, 36)), just as is the case in his own stories. What Borges specifically borrowed from Chesterton was the idea of detective stories with an implicit philosophical or metaphysical dimension. But while to Chesterton we owe the evolution of the genre from dealing with the obscure to dealing with the (apparently) inexplicable — which introduces the possibility of a symbolic parallelism with existence as we nowadays tend to see it — Chesterton himself as a dogmatic Catholic drew back from the full consequences of the development which he had perfected. Not so Borges, the neat design of whose detective stories hardly conceals his vision of a reality as unintelligible as the contents of the books in the Library of Babel.

At first sight 'La muerte y la brújula' seems to belong to a different category of story from that to which, say, 'La Biblioteca de Babel' belongs. The obvious difference is its very cunningly articulated plot, a factor which is lacking in the more directly symbolic stories. But Ronald Christ reminds us (9, 120) that this difference is largely illusory since 'for Borges the "mechanism of the detective story" and the "mechanism of the essay" are identical'. Properly understood, that is, Lönnrot's quest is not altogether different from that of the student in 'Almotásim' or that of the seekers in the Library of Babel. Hence the underlying structure of 'La muerte y la brújula' is once more tripartite. The opening posits a problem, indicates divergent reactions to it and promises a solution. The centre of the story develops the problem and describes the quest for an answer to it. The ending provides this answer in an unexpected and ambiguous way.

A feature of the narrative organization is the very prominent centre of balance, almost in the exact middle of the tale, marked by the arrival of Scharlach's letter and diagram. Up to this point the plot follows a conventional pattern of increasing complexity. A note-worthy aspect of this is the play which Borges makes with clues involving either three or four elements. The three crimes occur on the third of the month; Yarmolinsky is attending the third Talmudic Congress, the harlequins' costumes have three colours, and so on. On the other hand the crimes, by Jewish reckoning, took place on the fourth day of each month, the rhombs and lozenge shapes are four-sided and the words tetragrammaton and Tetrarch each suggest the number four. Similarly Treviranus' remark 'No hay que buscarle tres [*sic*, not as normally 'cinco'] pies al gato' calls to mind a cat's *four* legs. The climax of this alternation appears when Lönnrot, to his cost, converts the apparently complete equilateral triangle on Scharlach's map into a lozenge. This is one of Borges' most impressively elaborate technical effects.

There are two more elements which are of technical interest. One is the use of symbolic colours. First the grey beard and grey eyes of the doomed Yarmolinsky (cf. the 'hombre gris' of 'Las ruinas circulares'). Then yellow, beginning with the yellow waters of the estuary and continuing with the yellow rhombs, the yellow — and circular — moon, and the yellow colours of the furniture, all suggestive of sinister implications which are fulfilled at the end of the tale. We recall the 'yellow and black' garden of Stephen Albert in 'El jardín de senderos que se bifurcan'. The other element is the fact that the story is told entirely by an omniscient narrator. This is a very exceptional narrative method for Borges. His narrators, as T. E. Lyon points out (*28*, 363-72), usually invade the stories to contradict Borges himself, to cast doubt on the veracity of what is told or to mislead the reader, but always to create a bond of intimacy with him and to encourage him to take the story he is reading on trust.

Meanwhile the mystery deepens from incident to incident until Lönnrot is able to hint to Treviranus and to the reader that the clue to the solution lies in 'una palabra que dijo Ginzberg'. This is the point of maximum complexity. After a deliberate pause the letter and the map arrive and the clue-word (Tetragrammaton, i.e. a sacred word of four letters such as the Hebrew form of the word Jehovah) is revealed. Now the main originality of the story begins to become manifest. Normally the initiative would pass at this stage from the criminal to the detective and the arrest follow inexorably. Instead the story goes into reverse: the explanation is unfolded, but the criminal remains in command. The detective, instead of being led by a series of clues to the solution of the crime, is led to his own murderer.

At first sight, then, this is simply an ingenious detective story turned inside out. However, D. P. Gallagher, in a perceptive chapter of his book on modern Latin-American literature, warns us to concentrate our attention on the deeper level of meaning. Gallagher convincingly reads the story as 'a cautionary tale about the vanity of the intellect' (*38*, 98). The elements of *aventurero* and *tahur* in Lönnrot's make-up are necessary to justify his lone trip at the end of the story, but the key-phrase is 'Lönnrot se creía un puro razonador'. In contrast to the more straightforwardly commonsensical Treviranus, whose perfectly correct explanation of the original crime he impatiently brushes aside, Lönnrot jumps to the more rationally satisfying conclusion that Yarmolinsky's murder is a ritual sacrifice, the work of a Jewish Hassidic sect. He thereby delivers himself into the hands of Scharlach; he is deceived because of his reason. In this sense, then, the story is as Gallagher observes 'an amused critique of pure reason' (*38*, 101).

The same critic goes on to examine two more interpretations. The first, which Borges has hinted at, suggests that Lönnrot and Red Scharlach (as their respective names are intended to imply) are the same person.[7] Hence the duplication of identical architectural features in the house at Triste-le-Roy. The story thus becomes a metaphor of suicide. Underlying it are Borges' involvement with the idea of 'all men being one man or one man being his own mortal foe' (*7*, 130) and his quasi-obsession with circular time or the notion of Eternal Return. Hence Lönnrot's remark at the end: 'cuando en otro avatar usted me dé caza'. A problem of this interpretation is the absence of motive for Lönnrot's suicide, unless it be that excess of rationalism leads to the death-wish.

The second interpretation discussed by Gallagher suggests that Scharlach represents or symbolizes God. Relevant here are Scharlach's apparent omniscience and the three-fold name he gives at the tavern in the rue de Toulon, which is possibly a parody of the Trinity. The quest for the agent of events is the quest for God. The idea of an ironic God luring man on by deceitful signs, which suggest the possibility of organizing experience into an intelligible pattern, only to kill him at the last, is not entirely in disaccord with Borges' death-oriented and sceptical outlook. L. A. Middleman develops a kindred interpretation, but with Scharlach as Satan (*39*). However it may be, Lönnrot certainly symbolizes man, led by his reason into a labyrinth (whose complexity is, perhaps, partly subjective) from which death

---

[7] *The Aleph and Other Stories* (New York and London, 1970), 269.

alone releases him. The labyrinth, here as elsewhere (e.g. in the Library of Babel), represents reality as the rational mind sees it: a construct (but whose?) with an apparently purposive design, which however proves to be merely a bewildering trap, a more frightening modern equivalent of the prison-house image so dear to the Romantics. From this point of view Lönnrot's quest can be seen as another variation on the Borgesian theme of the impossible task.

One of the main problems in any symbolic interpretation is Scharlach himself. If the story is concerned with reason's struggle with reality, Scharlach is too active to be a suitable symbol for the latter. He implies the existence of an operative anti-force opposed to reason, when all that reality does is to resist rational comprehension passively, or else to mould itself to such comprehension in a deceitful way, as we saw in relation to Tlön where reality appears to accept the deformation which the act of perceiving it imposes on it. All this forces the recognition that Scharlach must be in some sense Lönnrot so that the two symbolize reason inevitably defeating itself. Lönnrot comes to grief by refusing to see what Treviranus (common sense) sees, and what Borges himself in 'La lotería en Babilonia' implies that the world is like. In this last connection the intervention of chance (cf. Scharlach's admission: 'El primer término de la serie me fue dado por el azar') corresponds to the chance which causes Dahlmann's train to stop at a different station in 'El Sur'.

Finally we may notice that the two contrasted figures, the rhomb and the straight line at the end of the tale, are possible symbols of the futility of Lönnrot's quest. The rhomb, which Borges presumably preferred to the line because the latter, although a more obvious symbol of the road of life, might suggest purposive forward movement, points in all four main directions, that is, nowhere. The line, in fact, is not a real alternative, for Lönnrot's idea is that it should eventually double back on itself not once, but twice, suggesting, one might almost say, a backward spiral.

What is finally impressive about 'La muerte y la brújula' is the way in which its manifold contrivances inter-connect and function harmoniously both at the straight narrative level and on the symbolic plane. It is unquestionably one of Borges' supreme fictional artifacts. Not until a decade later, with the publication of 'El Sur', was he to surpass it.

*El milagro secreto*

Practically every serious critic of Borges has recognized that time is one of his major recurrent preoccupations. He himself has confessed: 'I have always been obsessed by time' (*10*, 57). Time is one of the most complex elements in his work. His treatment of it has been examined from diametrically opposite points of view by Barrenechea and Blanco González. But more useful than either in relation to 'El milagro secreto', the most time-centred story of *Ficciones*, is the essay by Bagby: 'The Concept of Time in J. L. Borges'. Bagby notes that just as Borges goes beyond Berkeley in regard to the reality of matter, so he goes beyond both Berkeley and Hume in his negation of time. 'Borges is correct', according to Bagby, 'in pointing out that if outside each awareness (actual or conjectural) matter does not exist; and if also outside of each mental awareness the spirit does not exist, neither will time exist outside of each present moment.' Thus 'Borges thinks of every instant as autonomous'. 'Eternity, on the other hand', Bagby concludes (on the evidence of the famous passage 'Sentirse en muerte'), 'being limitless time, is the present stopped' (*17*, 103). Stabb points out that several of Borges' poems in the 1920s 'illustrate [his] intense desire to check the flow of time', to find a *remanso* in it (*3*, 35-6).

The relation of this to 'El milagro secreto' is obvious. In one sense, like 'El Sur', it is a story of wish-fulfilment. If each moment is autonomous, each moment potentially contains eternity, and there is a part of Borges which yearns for it. Equally Borges has frequently referred to his writings as the justification for his existence. In this story Hladík, like Menard earlier, shows a suspicious similarity to Borges himself. The reference to his *Vindicación de la eternidad* is plainly intended to recall Borges' *Historia de la eternidad*, while the reference to 'una antología de 1924' brings to mind *Indice de la nueva poesía americana* (1926), the first anthology which established Borges' reputation as a poet outside a narrow circle of readers. Hladík is granted a moment of eternity specifically to justify himself, that is, to impose a finality on his life and thereby on all life. By so doing he would convert aimless flux into divine design and thereby 'justify' God as well. Alas, however, this is a *ficción*. What is more, Hladík's drama dies with him. In terms of the story, the miracle is

known only to Hladík and God; it is not so much a secret miracle as
a pointless one, since nothing remains to testify to it. 'An unassuming
miracle', Borges called it (7, 38). The interest of 'El milagro secreto',
then, in relation to Borges' general outlook lies in the contrast which
is established between the search for finality via creative work and its
inevitable frustration. In this respect the story is closely related in its
implications to 'Pierre Menard'. Both Hladík and Menard 'succeed'
in fulfilling their aspirations. But in each case nothing remains to
attest their success. While this is unimportant superficially, at the
deeper level at which their aspirations symbolize respectively man's
desire to prove the existence of material reality and his longing for
finality, Menard's text and Hladík's death in the moment of his
creative fulfilment are of obvious negative significance.

The technical problem facing Borges in 'El milagro secreto' is once
more that of effecting the transition from the typically realistic
opening, with its deliberately obtrusive, concrete details of time and
place, to the supernatural conclusion. The story has four parts: the
circumstantial introduction dealing with Hladík and his arrest by the
Gestapo; his play 'Los enemigos'; his prayer and God's reply; and the
miracle. The opening is a classic example of Borges' meticulous construction of his tales. To Irby he explained that he had included the
dream of a chess game lasting for generations 'to obtain an effect of
contrast' with the culmination of the story when in a single instant
Hladík completes his entire play (25, 394). Possibly, since Hladík is
of Jewish blood, the game alludes to the age-old conflict of Jews and
Gentiles. We cannot fail to notice too that the general theme of conflict implicit in the chess game persists in Hladík's play and cannot be
dissociated from the context of the Second World War in which the
story as a whole is set. The secret tower, a symbol as we saw in
'Almotásim' of circularity and futility, in which the chess is played,
emphasizes the endlessness and pointlessness of all human conflicts.
But within this pattern of reference is another, in which Hladík is
struggling with time in a bewildering and contradictory situation ('un
desierto lluvioso') to make a move according to rules he cannot
remember, which may in the end produce an enormous and possibly
infinite prize. This aspect of the game obliquely foreshadows his
subsequent arrest, his prayer and its reward. The double effect of
contrast with, and anticipation of, events which Borges thus achieves

is strikingly impressive.

The ten days' delay, emphasized by the very precise time-notations, between Hladík's arrest and his execution produces a pause in the story. It allows Borges, through Hladík's reflections, to insinuate to the reader two ideas: first, that to imagine in detail a future event is to prevent its occurrence (i.e. to modify the future by an act of imagination); second, that to be alive, but under sentence of death, is to achieve a semblance of immortality. Both ideas involve an element of triumph over time by the imagination, underlined by the reference to Hladík's longing to 'afirmarse de algún modo en la sustancia fugitiva del tiempo'. Further hints of the possibility of such a triumph are contained in the reference to Hladík's *Vindicación de la eternidad.*

Hladík's play *Los enemigos* already existed in Borges' mind before he began writing the story. 'I had also thought out the idea of a drama in two acts', he told Burgin, 'and in the first act you would have something very noble and rather pompous, and then in the second act you would find that the real thing was rather tawdry' (7, 38). Perhaps this is a hint about how we are to view the story as a whole: as the story of a tawdry miracle. More importantly, *Los enemigos* concerns time. Just as Ts'ui Pên's novel in 'El jardín de senderos que se bifurcan' contained the idea of multiple time sequences, so here time is at once immobile and circular. The play, that is, develops artistically the theory expressed by Hladík in the second volume of his *Vindicación de la eternidad*, that not all events necessarily occur in a single time sequence. The alert reader is now sensitized to the idea of time as protean, and is thus psychologically prepared for the miracle. At the same time the references to Hebrew writings, with the implication of a hidden language discoverable in reality, and through it a magical mode of communication with God, prepare the response to Hladík's prayer.

Like Ts'ui Pên's novel, *Los enemigos* is a work of imagination inside a work of imagination. The general significance of such reduplication for Borges was alluded to earlier, apropos of 'Las ruinas circulares'. Specifically, however, we notice that, just as Ts'ui Pên's work is intrinsically related to the rest of Yu Tsun's story, so *Los enemigos* is to Hladík's. Ts'ui Pên's novel foreshadows and in a sense contains the conflict between Yu Tsun and Albert as well as the wider

conflict, the war, within which this last is set. *Los enemigos*, apart
from its stopped time, is connected with Hladík's situation by hints
of conflict and death but above all by the fact that it takes place in
Kubin's mind only. Hladík is mentally conceiving an unreal series of
events (his play), in which Kubin is mentally conceiving an unreal
series of events (his delirium). The stopping of time applies equally
to both. While interior reduplication shakes our faith in our own
reality, this particular instance of interior reduplication underlines the
theme of the story as well: that time is no less subject than other
aspects of reality to the possibility that it exists only in the mind.

Here we have the counterbalance to Borges' idea of existence as a
labyrinth with no centre, or nothing at the centre, and only death as
an exit. It is the idea of the world as a cryptogram, with the possibility of stumbling on the clue which will explain it. Both ideas were
present in 'La Biblioteca de Babel'. But here, as in 'La escritura del
Dios' (*El Aleph*) and in Borges' 'Poema conjetural' (1943, i.e. about
the same time as the story), it is the latter which is uppermost. Just
as Laprida in the poem discovers:

> la letra que faltaba, la perfecta
> forma que supo Dios desde el principio  (OP, 149)

so Hladík finds a magic letter in a name on a map and God answers
his prayer.

In the ending two elements previously hinted at, the malleability
of time and the idea of a magic clue, are brought together. At the
same time Hladík undergoes an experience vaguely prefigured in his
own writings (cf. the denial of temporal sequence in *Vindicación de
la eternidad* and the stopped clock in *Los enemigos*) in a way which
suggests, like 'Tema del traidor y del héroe' and in a different way
'Tlön, Uqbar, Orbis Tertius', that reality is somehow permeable to
the imagination. But the ending itself remains ambiguous. Borges'
statement that it concerns 'a religious idea, of a man justifying himself to God by something known only to God, no? God giving him
his chance' (7, 38), provokes the question: Giving him his chance to
do what? To write a play which, like Ts'ui Pên's novel, is a labyrinth, a circular delirium, a dream within a dream. The idea of self-
justification through writing is counterbalanced by the theme of the
writing itself, which is futility. This is one of Borges' impasses.

## El fin

Dauster (*20*, 145) suggests that the key to 'El fin' is to be found in an essay on Beowulf in *Antiguas literaturas germánicas* (1955) where Borges wrote:

Hay pocos argumentos posibles; uno de ellos es el del hombre que da con su destino. (24)

On the same page Borges interprets Beowulf as the story of:

un hombre que cree haber sido vencedor en una batalla y que después de muchos años tiene que librarla otra vez y no es vencedor. Sería la fábula de un hombre a quien alcanza finalmente el destino y de una batalla que vuelve.

Borges' remark in the *prólogo* to *Artificios* about 'un libro famoso' on which 'El fin' is based refers to José Hernández's great poem of gaucho life *Martín Fierro*, published in two parts in 1872 and 1878. Here we seem to have, then, an adaptation of the story of Martín Fierro to bring it into line with this pattern. The appeal to Borges of such an adaptation is obvious, since it unites the two great epics of British and Argentine literature in a way which at the same time involves the idea of eternal return: Fierro becomes a modern avatar of Beowulf. Wheelock interprets the story as being basically about the end of the poetic ambiguity inherent in the rivalry between Fierro and the negro (*28*, 376). 'Fierro's death puts an end to the poetic tension; the remaining gaucho cannot embody the transcendent, unformulated idea, and the "imminence" is lost.' But the problem of the relation between the fight and its setting remains. Perhaps, like Borges' later story 'Pedro Salvadores', 'El fin' has to do with destiny as something which, the author says, 'strikes us as a symbol of something we are about to understand, but never quite do' (*26*, 78).

The destiny which overtakes Fierro in 'El fin' is markedly different from the destiny which awaits Dahlmann in 'El Sur' as he leaves the store with his opponent, or the destiny which reveals itself to Cruz in 'Biografía de Tadeo Isidoro Cruz in *El Aleph*. Destiny for Dahlmann and Cruz reveals itself in a climactic moment of illumination and fulfilment, in which each suddenly comes to the centre of his own private existential labyrinth and discovers the meaning of his own existence. Here on the other hand destiny is seen anti-climactically: when its hour strikes, nothing essential changes.

Hence the story begins, not with Fierro but with Recabarren, the helplessly paralysed, resigned, stoic onlooker. His paralysis, like that of Funes, is the physical concomitant of lucidity. He represents the human mind, impotent and dumb, but 'sufrido', in the face of existence, which it can contemplate but not understand or alter. His detached immobility balances the futile drama enacted in front of him. This immobility is not only physical but also spiritual, since, like the cat whom Dahlmann envies, Recabarren lives only in the present moment. The meaning of the drama is symbolized in the negro's guitar-music: 'una suerte de pobrísimo laberinto que se enredaba y desataba infinitamente.' Recabarren is also Schopenhauer's man of insight, who has turned away from action and involvement and thus liberated himself spiritually from life's squalid labyrinth. Fierro and the negro are trapped inside it. They are differentiated by their respective levels of insight. Fierro knows himself to have been trapped since he first shed blood. He accepts along with his own guilt the iron law of fatality by which one act of violence inevitably generates another. He hints that only an act of renunciation on the part of his antagonist can break the chain. To do more than hint would imply fear. The negro however is intent on vengeance. He sees the encounter with Fierro as a solution, not as a minute element in the infinite series of entanglements and disentanglements which we call life. And yet, ironically, as an artist (a musician) he was unconsciously expressing such a vision of existence through his playing while waiting for Fierro to arrive. Thus three levels of awareness are presented in the story's opening in a descending order: Recabarren's, Fierro's and the negro's. The latter's words to Fierro as they go out: 'Tal vez en éste me vaya tan mal como en el primero' [i.e. in the song-contest] are no less ironically prophetic than his music. Apparently he wins; but in fact all that he has done is to release Fierro from the trap and enter it consciously himself.

The story's technique has familiar elements. The narrator is actually omniscient, a point emphasized by the curiously un-Borgesian last two sentences of the tale, which are straight commentary. He pretends, however, not to know a factual detail: the relationship between Recabarren and the boy. Borges has admitted (*10*, 45) that this is one of his favourite narrative devices, designed to create credibility. The 'red' moon is another example of the same colour-symbolism which was noticed in 'La muerte y la brújula'. Probably it suggests here the imminence of violence. The sense of being on the brink of a revelation (which never comes), that Borges refers to just before the fight itself, is similar to the stationary moment experienced by Yu Tsun just before he hears the music in Albert's house. Fierro's *cansancio*, the weariness of acquired insight, is also shared by Yu Tsun. The chief feature, however, is the skilfully arranged shift in the story from the symbolism and immobilism of the opening to the dramatic climax. It is achieved this time through dialogue, a very rare feature of Borges' stories. Until the negro's last speech, which reveals the cause of the enmity, the conversation is carefully de-dramatized and the hostility of the interlocutor expressed only in indirect allusions. Similarly Fierro's identity is concealed until the same moment. The double revelation is at once followed by the fight and the concluding comments. The opening phrase of the concluding sentence, 'Mejor dicho era el otro', reaffirms the idea which underlies 'La forma de la espada' and is also present in 'La muerte y la brújula'; the idea, that is, that each man is everyman, that the victim is in some way his killer, that guilt is reversible. Critics have argued about whether Borges' tales grow out of existing literary prefigurations of them or whether they grow out of metaphysical ideas. 'El fin' plainly grew out of both.

## La secta del Fénix

'La secta del Fénix', perhaps the least important, but one of the most charming, stories in *Ficciones*, is simply an elaborate joke. It was suggested, according to Ronald Christ, by De Quincey's essay 'Secret Societies'. Borges himself confessed to this critic what most readers at once suspect: that the sect is mankind generally, and that the secret rite which unites its members is the sexual act. The reference to cork, wax and gum is a red herring. Perhaps the best comment on this tale is Rodríguez Monegal's remark that in it Borges 'elevates euphemism to allegory'.

## El Sur

'El Sur' occupies a special position in *Ficciones* not only because it closes the volume but also because its realistic setting combined with an ambiguous element of fantasy gives it a distinctly different

tone from the preceding stories. The fact that Borges described it in
the prologue to *Artificios* as 'acaso mi mejor cuento' is of major
importance. In 1971 he stated: ' "The South" is really a story of
wishful thinking' and went on to suggest: 'Actually there are several
plots. One of them might be that the man [i.e. Dahlmann] died on
the operating table, and that the whole thing was a dream of his, in
which he was striving to get the death he wanted. I mean, he wanted
to die with a knife in his hand on the pampa; he wanted to die fighting
as his forefathers had fought before him' (*10*, 50).

'El Sur' in fact can be read in one of at least three ways. The first
and most essential way is to read it simply as a story, remembering
Borges' impatience with people who are 'always looking for some
kind of lesson' in his work. At this level, as he said on the same
occasion, 'The tale itself should be its own reality' (*7*, 66-7). At this
level the critic's only task is that of clarifying the technical means by
which the tale succeeds. But this does not preclude other approaches.
The second way to read 'El Sur' is in relation to Borges himself,
whose life 'infested with literature' has been dogged by what he
referred to as 'my yearning after that epic destiny which my gods
denied me' (*1*, 42). The third way is to see the story as in some way
symbolizing the search for national identity which has been a prominent feature of Argentine and Latin-American literature generally.
Perhaps, even, we may also perceive in the story a reflection of man's
search for his own identity. Zunilda Gertel, in the fullest analysis so
far published of 'El Sur', assumes rather arbitrarily that Dahlmann's
journey must be a death-bed hallucination and sees it as containing
'El sentido simbólico trascendente del cuento' (*40*, 39). Dahlmann,
that is, identifies himself ultimately with his maternal grandfather
Francisco Flores and finds the centre of his personal labyrinth in an
act which is a repetition, in a sense, of the latter's fate. Stripped of
its too obtrusive structuralist jargon, Gertel's essay contains extremely
useful insights into Borges' subtle narrative method in this story.

On one level, then, 'El Sur' can be read as a story which belongs to
those in which Borges, from 'Hombre de la esquina rosada' on,
revealed his admiration of courage, especially when expressed in
duelling with knives.[8] The ending illustrates his belief in the moment

---

[8] Cf. in this connection L.A. Gyurko's useful article 'Borges and the *Machismo*
Cult', *Revista Hispánica Moderna*, XXXVI (1970-71), 128-45.

of self-discovery which is referred to in 'Biografía de Tadeo Isidoro Cruz': 'Cualquier destino, por largo y complicado que sea, consta en realidad *de un solo momento*: el momento en que el hombre sabe para siempre quién es' (A, 55). This is Dahlmann's discovery at the story's climax.

At a second level Dahlmann can be partly identified with Borges. Like Borges he is of mixed North-European and distinguished Argentine ancestry. He, too, is a librarian, is unassumingly patriotic and adores *The Arabian Nights*. Most of all he, too, suffers a head injury followed by septicaemia. Borges has shown unequivocal signs of regret that the military, heroic tradition of his family has played no part in his life. Dahlmann's death in a knife-fight on the pampa is in a sense a vicarious event expressing Borges' dream of death in action like the death of his own grandfather Colonel Francisco Borges in 1874.

Finally Dahlmann's end can be seen as symbolizing his achieve-ment of *Argentinidad*. His death in true gaucho fashion crowns the deliberate choice of *criollo* allegiance mentioned in the opening para-graph of the tale. The old gaucho, with his anachronistic *chiripá* and *botas de potro*, who throws him the knife, represents as it were the *alma de la raza* offering him the chance to put his allegiance to the supreme test. The fact that Dahlmann does so chiefly because his name has been mentioned publicly in connection with the *peón*'s provocation links his *Argentinidad* to the wider context of *Hispani-dad* through the tradition of *pundonor*.

The main technical feature of the story is its ambiguity. From the beginning of the third paragraph (the clue is the word *simetrías*, i.e. coincidences, which is intended to alert us to the fact that the rest of the story may be unreal) we do not know whether the events des-cribed happen as they appear to happen or represent a dream in Dahlmann's mind. Phillips, Christ, Gertel and Hall have each analyzed the structure of the tale showing how its parts are linked together by a subtly organized series of correlations hinting at the possibility that Dahlmann's journey is a hallucination. They are based on elements already present during his stay in the clinic. Hall makes the valid point that we cannot, in fact, be certain when the hallucination, if such it is, begins. It could begin with the onset of Dahlmann's fever while he is still at home and thus render the whole of the story after the opening a hallucination. Equally it could begin in the train as a dream while Dahlmann sleeps. In Hall's view we cannot exclude the possibility that the story is a multiple structure, like Ts'ui Pên's novel, with several possible outcomes. At all events the cab in which Dahlmann travels to the station reminds him of one which he had taken to the clinic; the book he reads on the train is the one he was carrying when he received his injury — its title suggests unreality as we saw in connection with the use of the number 1001 in 'Tlön, Uqbar, Orbis Tertius' and 'Las ruinas circulares'; the owner of the store reminds him of a male nurse; the pellet of bread strikes his head like the edge of the door which originally produced his wound; finally the knife-wound from which Dahlmann expects to die is compared to the hypodermic needle which had freed him from pain. Perhaps most conclusively of all, the store-keeper, a stranger, addresses him by name. Thus we can explain the reference to 'dos hombres' in the ninth paragraph and the repetition of *elegir/soñar: elegido/soñado* in the penultimate sentence.

To these correlations and others suggested by Gertel are added a series of faint ironies designed to sharpen the impact of the ending. Dahlmann's journey is undertaken in the belief that it is a journey away from death, which had threatened him in the clinic, towards convalescence and renewal of life; in fact Dahlmann is travelling to meet death. His joy at opening *The Arabian Nights* on the train is a challenge to 'las frustradas fuerzas del mal', which in fact are only too operative. The subsequent remark: 'se dejaba simplemente vivir' is the prelude to violent death. Two more features of the technique merit mention. One is the tiny intervention of chance which results in Dahlmann's being set down at a different station and thus determines his death. His train ticket is in this respect yet another ticket in the *Lotería en Babilonia*. The other is the use of the cat-symbol at the beginning of the tale's second part. The cat, ensconced in a perpetual present, is beyond time and hence beyond death: it partakes already of eternity. The contrast with Dahlmann, trapped inside time, which is about to run out for him, accentuates the fact of his belonging to the human condition; it lifts him momentarily onto the universal plane. His conscious awareness of the contrast provides the overwhelming irony of the story: destiny is about to prove the tragic relevance of that awareness. Gertel also effectively demonstrates the technical importance of the way in which Borges shifts the narrator's position relative to Dahlmann from one which is external and impersonal to that of virtually complete identification with him. She stresses also Borges' alternation of chronological and psychic time in the story, and the stages into which Dahlmann's journey to the South can be divided, ending with 'el alcance de la otra orilla . . . el conocimiento de los secretos tránsitos del laberinto' (*40*, 43).

'El Sur' brings *Ficciones* to an appropriate end. Courage and self-discovery, the achievement of personal *autenticidad* seem to triumph in the moment of death. Yet the reader is left with the uneasy sensation that all may be merely a sick fantasy. The centre of the labyrinth may exist only as a wishful dream.

In an interview quoted by Barrenechea Borges said: 'I have always been sluggish in writing; each phrase has always presented itself under various guises: before arriving at a word I have to go through many synonyms and choose from a variety of metaphors' (*5*, 151). This enormously meticulous concept of style, involving draft after draft for each paragraph, accounts for the compactness, precision and slightly mannered elegance of Borges' prose. It stands apart both from the 'orfebrería verbal', the self-consciously artistic prose, of the *modernistas* and their immediate successors, over-stuffed with deliberate poetic devices as it became in Lugones' *La guerra gaucha* for instance, and from the often banal narrative expression of writers in the realist or 'documental' tradition such as Azuela or Ciro Alegría. Borges certainly began to write under the former influence, but rapidly grew out of it. 'When I began to write', he tells us in the same interview, 'I searched for astounding epithets and metaphors, while now [1960] I feel that astonishment must be avoided and that everything must be facilitated for the reader.' Another occasional feature of his earlier style was his deliberate use of argentinisms. But this too was outgrown. 'I don't want to write like a Spaniard', he told Keith Botsford, 'at the same time it would be an awful mistake if I tried consciously and conscientiously to write like an Argentinian' (*19*, 729).

A few attempts have been made, notably by Barrenechea and Alazraki, to describe or analyze Borges' style. Some conclusions may be mentioned. The most important concerns Borges' use of adjectives. We notice, for example, accumulations of adjectives in sentences like 'Era el *solitario* y *lúcido* espectador de un mundo *multiforme, instantáneo* y casi intolerablemente *preciso*' (F, 126), or '*Minucioso, inmóvil, secreto*, urdió en el tiempo su *alto* laberinto *invisible*' (F, 167), or 'La Biblioteca perdurará: *iluminada, solitaria, infinita,* perfectamente *inmóvil,* armada de volúmenes *preciosos, inútil, incorruptible, secreta*' (F, 95). Many of the adjectives which Borges thus employs, always deliberately and consciously, very often placed before the noun to gain emphasis, tend to recur frequently and hence take on special significance because of what their consistent use reveals about his outlook. Such Borgesian key-adjectives include: *infinito, vasto, remoto, circular, inextricable, caótico, perplejo, enigmático* and *vertiginoso*. Along with them goes a class of adjectives and expressions which imply vagueness, indeterminacy, doubt, fallibility and insecurity, such as: *vago, mero, inútil, torpe, negligente* and *ilusorio*. The colour grey belongs to this category too. So does Borges' use of expressions in parenthesis, or between commas or dashes, to imply hesitancy as to the right way to express what he is referring to, e.g: 'Yo tenía el temor (la esperanza) . . . ' (F, 118); [Funes] 'razonó (sintió)' (F, 123); or more obviously [Hladík] 'afrontaba con verdadero terror (quizá con verdadero coraje)' (F, 161). Here Borges is deliberately attenuating the impression of authorial omniscience. 'I think one should work into a story the idea of not being sure of all things, because that's the way reality is', he explained (*10*, 45). A different kind of vagueness sometimes surrounds the physical environment of his stories so as to produce a dream-like effect. An example is 'el vago y vivo campo' with its 'confusas praderas' in which Albert's house stands (F, 102). Afternoons seem propitious for this effect of blurred outlines; that in which Yu Tsun finds himself is 'íntima, infinita'. In 'El fin', time of day and countryside are blended together by the single verb, '*se dilataban* la llanura y la tarde' (F, 177), into one infinite extension. The afternoon in 'La muerte y la brújula' which hangs over 'la *turbia* llanura' in contrast offers a vague symmetry with the events which follow: 'Era una de esas tardes desiertas que parecen amaneceres' (F, 152). Its ambiguity portends the dashing of Lönnrot's hopes of vanquishing Scharlach.

Certain juxtapositions of adjectives without a preposition to mark the contrast are also typical: 'la luz que emiten es *insuficiente, incesante*' (F, 86): 'Una sola línea recta . . . *invisible, incesante*' (F, 158). More emphatically antithetical is the reference to 'una realidad *atroz* o *banal*' (F, 13) at the end of a very long sentence, which includes a parenthetical use of dashes, to produce an ironically anticlimactic effect. A similar instance is the description of Menard's task as 'complejísimo' and 'fútil'. Indeed ironic use of adjectives is rather prominent, as in the case of 'el *divino* desorden' (F, 91); 'mi *deplorable* condición de argentino' (F, 117); 'no merecen tal vez la *continua* atención de *todos* los hombres' (F, 20) or 'es *verosímil* que esos graves misterios pueden explicarse en palabras' (F, 91). A more simply humorous example is the final word in Borges' description of the Indian police: 'atronadora, ecuestre, *semidormida*' (F, 37). There are also a great many transferred epithets, in which the emotion or impression provoked by a thing is attached to the thing itself: 'una cicatriz *rencorosa*' (F, 129); 'una *indecisa* traducción' (F, 34); 'la *íntima* casa' (F, 103). Oxymoron, or contradictory-sounding adjectivization, such as 'pasividad laboriosa' (F, 153) and 'desiertos lluviosos' (F, 159), is not uncommon. A few individual adjectives have extra-special meaning in their context. The most famous is 'unánime' in the first line of 'Las ruinas circulares' (cf. p. 26, above). Another occurs in the reference to 'una oscura pasionaria' (F, 117) in the third line of 'Funes el memorioso'; it is obscure to us, that is, but not to Funes, who sees it 'como nadie la ha visto'. The single adjective again prefigures the entire theme of the story. The colour yellow seems to have its usual sinister associations, and critics including Gertel have noticed that the adjective 'vertiginoso' and cognate expressions are often closely connected with fatal moments or decisions in Borges' stories. They thus become a kind of call-sign of particular significance.

Symbolic or semi-symbolic nouns such as *laberinto, red, espejo, torre, sueño, caos, fantasma* and *vértigo* abound. Again, nouns are often curiously juxtaposed, as in: 'A todo padre le interesan los hijos que ha procreado (que ha permitido) [once more a characteristic parenthesis] en una mera *confusión* o *felicidad*' (F, 65). Verbs can be unexpected, not always felicitously, as in: 'una lámpara *ilustraba* [instead of *iluminaba*] el andén' (F, 101). But contrast: 'hondas descargas de artillería *conmovieron* el Sur' (F, 133) and 'El espejo *inquietaba* el fondo de un corredor . . . el espejo nos *acechaba*' (F, 13).

Similes and metaphors are rare. We notice in *Ficciones*: 'el cielo que tenía el color rosado de la encía de los leopardos' close to 'las humaredas que herrumbraron el metal de las noches' (F, 66), a very uncommon example of successive metaphors. Elsewhere in the text we find: 'el sueño le anegó como una agua oscura' (F, 164), and 'Moon estaba inmóvil, fascinado y como eternizado por el terror' (F, 132), phrases which stand out stiffly from the prose because of their figurative language. More common rhetorical devices are repetition: 'Con alivio, con humillación, con terror' (F, 66); 'Como todos . . .

como todos . . . Miren . . . Miren . . .' (F, 67); 'Recuerdo . . . Recuerdo . . . Recuerdo . . .' (F, 117) [six times in all] ; and alliteration: 'me mostró con débil dulzura la corva cicatriz blanquecina' (F, 135); 'me sentía visible y vulnerable, infinitamente' (F, 100).

It is hazardous, however, to generalize about Borges' fictional style. The same story can contain very different kinds of prose. A case in point is 'La forma de la espada'. Its opening paragraph merely contains a succession of unadorned statements, separated by colons, semi-colons and full stops. In nearly two hundred words the conjunction 'y' occurs only four times. The passage is stark and simple. Only the familiar string of adjectives, 'pálido, trémulo, azorado y tan autoritario como antes' (F, 129), modifies slightly the effect of close-packed information. But in the same story we find:

> El edificio tenía menos de un siglo, pero era desmedrado y opaco y abundaba en perplejos corredores y en vanas ante-cámaras. El museo y la enorme biblioteca usurpaban la planta baja: libros controversiales e incompatibles que de algún modo son la historia del siglo xix; cimitarras de Nishapur, en cuyos detenidos arcos de círculo parecían perdurar el viento y la violencia de la batalla. (F, 132)

Although it is supposed to belong to an oral narration, this is a tissue of stylistic devices. They include: the deliberate repetition of *y* in the first sentence; the characteristic adjectives *opaco, perplejos* and *vanas*; the unusual use of *usurpaban* and *incompatibles*; the following verb *son* rather than *contienen* (with the implication that the books are literally all that is left of the events); the striking metaphor which describes the curved scimitars; and finally the alliterations of the last clause.

Borges' mature fictional prose conveys an impression of extreme density of meaning combined with remarkable visuality. Yu Tsun's mental conversion of a seen object, a bird crossing the sky over his head, into a host of bombers fulfilling his plan and even his destiny (F, 98),in a sense symbolizes this unique combination. The style of *Ficciones, El Aleph* and later stories constitutes a supreme illustration of Ernesto Sábato's remark that: 'Un buen escritor expresa grandes cosas con pequeñas palabras; a la inversa del mal escritor, que dice cosas insignificantes con grandes palabras.'[9]

---

[9] *El escritor y sus fantasmas* (3rd ed., Buenos Aires, 1967), 209.

'If I am rich in anything, it is perplexities rather than certainties', Borges wrote in the prologue to his conversations with Burgin. His father was an atheist, his mother a practising Roman Catholic. He himself maintains an attitude of total agnosticism; but a scrutiny of his writings yields various examples of his gently ironic rejection of conventional Western conceptions of God and a number of critical remarks about Roman Catholicism in particular. He has categorically stated that references to God or to the divine in his work are to be regarded as formal devices only (cf., *inter alia, 12,* 144). The first result of this sceptical agnosticism is Borges' recognition that belief in the meaningfulness of existence becomes difficult to maintain. Once one accepts 'la imposibilidad de penetrar el esquema divino del universo' (OI, 143), the consequence tends to impose itself that 'Es dudoso que el mundo tenga sentido' (OI, 175). Secondly, as soon as complete scepticism is postulated, it naturally includes the postulator. Borges has no qualms about this. We ourselves are also a mystery: 'Los hombres gozan de poca información acerca de los móviles profundos de su conducta' (OI, 184). A third consequence of Borges' outlook is his awareness that we do not understand reality. If there is no God to guarantee the truth of our sense-impressions, if reason has failed to explain the mechanism of the universe and of our minds, then any confidence we may have in our ability to recognize and understand the really real is quite possibly unfounded.

If we do not understand life's significance, or ourselves, or the world in which we live, what follows? First, all combinations of experience are possible; nothing can be ruled out, for we have no fixed criterion. Anything, logical or illogical, can happen; any explanation, credible or incredible, may be true. Second, all things may be the result of pure chance, arbitrary and incomprehensible. Again, all things may be illusion. Equally, all may be unity. The world may be an infinite language of symbols which we have forgotten how to interpret or perhaps never knew how to decipher, but from which we can glean strange and intriguing hints of an ultimate pattern. All is conjecture. The world and reality become non-predictable, or perhaps predictable according to rules which we are used to regarding as absurd. Experience becomes a meaningless jumble, or a jumble which possibly contains mysterious suggestions or orderly recurrence which may imply meanings utterly different from accepted ones.

In his most original short stories Borges explores this outlook. He examines reality as if it were a strange and sometimes fearsome puzzle, but one which might yield certain inferences, clues or possible explanations. We can tentatively describe these stories as, in some sort, parables or fables illustrating the collapse of rational and fideistic certainties and the bewildering possibilities which thus emerge. Their humour is their main balancing factor. It is not the shrill and bitter humour generated by spiritual stress, but the expression of a detached, playful awareness of the absurdity of the human condition.

Most of the writing which has been done about Borges' work is, or attempts to be, expository and explanatory. Only one serious critic, Néstor Ibarra in *Cahiers l'Herne*, has ventured to criticize aspects of technique in certain stories by Borges, and these aspects are marginal ones. Hence Borges criticism has centred chiefly on issues which are more concerned with his outlook than with his actual fictional writings. Since many of his best stories are ultimately about ways of interpreting our experience, one question is: whether Borges' understanding of philosophy is adequate to support the metaphysical dimension these stories contain. Among others Ernesto Sábato, and especially M. Blanco González, have strong reservations on this score and tend to suggest, from a hostile *a priori* standpoint, that their criticisms at least partially invalidate what Borges seems to be saying about existence. Connected with this is the point that if 'la realidad no es verbal' Borges' attempt to say anything about it is wasted endeavour. The argument stands up logically while one thinks about it, but seems to fade away when we return to Borges' stories themselves. Another recurrent criticism asserts that Borges' work, which tends to deny or subvert exterior reality, is merely escapist and hence politically reactionary in its very essence. This is not an unreasonable criticism if one accepts the premiss that non-involvement in the politico-social struggle is on the writer's part the unforgivable sin. Borges has replied with the statement: 'I think a writer's duty is to be a writer, and if he can be a good writer, he is doing his duty ... I am an antagonist of *littérature engagée* because I think it stands on the hypothesis that a writer can't write what he wants to' (*10*, 59). Amid the welter of committed writing which is characteristic of modern Latin-American literature, his work remains detached. It is concerned not with advocating changes in social conditions, but with investigating the human condition. It is in the best sense exploratory. It stimulates the reader not to act or react, but to think. 'I am interested', Borges has said, 'in the fact of a man dedicating himself to his dreams, then trying to work them out. And doing his best to make other people share them.' (7, 128-9).

A final criticism is that Borges' cerebrality, the absence of emotion or deep ethical commitment, creates an impression of coldness and impersonality. Certainly his stories often appeal directly to the mind and to the mind only. In some cases their very form, as pseudo-reviews or articles, suggests that this is what Borges intended. This has to be accepted. Borges' greatest triumph is to produce, through the imaginative exploration of an initially odd-seeming idea, a genuine 'frisson métaphysique' in the reader. The art of Borges expresses tragedy without terror, awareness without undue anguish, existential bewilderment qualified by humour. Every choice, whether in art or life, involves a sacrifice. Borges' choice of approach in his fiction involves the sacrifice of our ability to identify ourselves emotionally with his characters. Only rarely, as when a note of heroism appears, does he forsake his attitude of detachment.

Borges' fiction stands at the opposite extreme from conventional realism. His stories can be seen as one of the peaks of the reaction in twentieth-century literature against the former tendency to idolize observed reality, bowing down even before its grosser aspects as before an absolute. Borges' use of the real as a springboard to launch his readers into the fantastic reasserts the rights of the creative imagination; but not just for its own sake. His aim is to uncover something more real than mere outward appearances: not beauty, which some of the first novelists of the reaction against realism in Spain believed was the alternative, but a possible aspect of truth. The accent lies on the word possible. Not for Borges to throw down one idol, observed reality, and set up another, beauty or truth. His way is subtler. He leads us away from such simple categories and ultimately impossible choices to acceptance, without undue preoccupation, of hypotheses which are outside the range of writers who remain tied to the problem of the real or the imaginary.

Critics disagree about whether Borges' world view is in the end positive, negative or neutral. It can be argued that his creation of a fantastic world inside our own world, operating according to certain imaginary laws, represents a triumph of art over the chaos of reality. Hence Ronald Christ's assertion that 'To produce a concentrated essential literature expressing a metaphysical apprehension of the fundamental and fantastic unity of life has been the basic goal of his major effects' (*9*, 97). Irby similarly supports the view that Borges 'questions the validity of [the] created world . . . in order to give it even greater reality, the reality of ideal construction' (*24*, 139), while Wheelock argues that what we have is Borges' 'idea that the creations of the mind are inevitably fraught with logical contradictions which prove their value and point beyond them to something yet unseen' (*15*, 95-6). My own view is that such statements do not set the case in quite the right light. We must bear in mind Borges' remark to Milleret — 'the consolation which the hypothesis of an unreal world offers',[10] — and his more famous 'El mundo, desgraciadamente, es real; yo, desgraciadamente, soy Borges' (OI, 256). I accept the view of Anderson Imbert that to Borges 'el mundo es un caos y que dentro de ese caos el hombre está perdido como en un laberinto'.[11]

There are hopeful signs, however, that criticism of Borges is moving away from such issues. The work of Gertel, Mills, Hall, Gallagher and others suggests that the way forward lies with close technical analysis of individual stories, similar in its methods and objectives to what is currently being published about single poems of, for example, Vallejo or Neruda. The present brief survey of *Ficciones* is chiefly indebted to this current of Borges criticism.

[10] 'Cette *consolation* qu'est l'hypothèse d'un monde irréel' (*12*, 102).

[11] *Crítica interna* (Madrid, 1960), 256; quoted by Alazraki.

# Bibliographical Note

## BIBLIOGRAPHY

The standard bibliography on Borges is Horacio Jorge Becco's *Jorge Luis Borges, Bibliografía total, 1923-1973* (Buenos Aires: Pardo, 1973). See also David William Foster, *Jorge Luis Borges: An Annotated Primary and Secondary Bibliography* (New York: Garland, 1984).

## TRANSLATION

*Ficciones* has been translated into English as *Fictions* by Anthony Kerrigan (London: Weidenfeld and Nicolson; New York: Grove Press, 1962).

## BIOGRAPHY

*1.* Borges, Jorge Luis, 'Autobiographical Notes', *New Yorker* (19 September 1970), 40-99. Also published in *The Aleph and Other Stories*, edited by Norman Thomas di Giovanni (New York: Dutton, 1970; London: Cape, 1971).
*2.* Jurado, Alicia, *Genio y figura de Jorge Luis Borges* (Buenos Aires: Editorial Universitaria, 1964). A general illustrated biography by a friend.
*2a.* Rodríguez Monegal, Emir, *Jorge Luis Borges. A Literary Biography* (New York: Dutton, 1978).

## GENERAL STUDIES

*2b.* McMurray, George R., *Jorge Luis Borges* (New York: Ungar, 1980). A good general survey.
*3.* Stabb, Martin S., *Jorge Luis Borges* (New York: Twayne, 1970). A good introduction to Borges' work as a whole.

## CRITICAL STUDIES

The only book, other than this Guide, wholly dedicated to *Ficciones* is *Borges, Fictions* (Paris: Edition Marketing, 1988), no editor named, containing more than twenty contributions in French, many on individual tales.

Other books include:

4. Alazraki, Jaime, *La prosa narrativa de Jorge Luis Borges* (Madrid: Gredos, 1968). An excellent study of themes and stylistic techniques.

4a. ———, *Versiones, inversiones, reversiones* (Madrid: Gredos, 1977). The first book to examine critically the structure of Borges' tales.

5. Barrenechea, Ana María, *Borges the Labyrinth Maker* (New York: New York U.P., 1965). Translated with additions from *La expresión de la irrealidad en la obra de Jorge Luis Borges* (Mexico City: El Colegio de México, 1957). Still the best critical introduction to Borges' fictional work.

5a. Bell-Villada, Gene H., *Borges and his Fiction: A Guide to his Mind and Art* (Chapel Hill: North Carolina U.P., 1981). Chiefly on content; pedestrian, but with some useful comments.

6. Blanco González, Manuel, *Jorge Luis Borges, anotaciones sobre el tiempo en su obra* (Mexico City: Di Andrea, 1963). Hostile. Considers Borges' views self-contradictory and frivolous.

7. Burgin, Richard, *Conversations with Jorge Luis Borges* (New York: Avon, 1968). Especially useful for comments by Borges on his own work.

8. Charbonnier, Georges, *Entretiens avec Jorge Luis Borges* (Paris: Gallimard, 1967). Also contains illuminating comments.

9. Christ, Ronald, *The Narrow Act: Borges' Art of Allusion* (New York: New York U.P., 1969). Very useful, especially on the development of Borges' fictional technique.

10. Di Giovanni, Norman Thomas, *et al., Borges on Writing* (New York: Dutton, 1973). See comment on 7.

11. Ferrer, Manuel, *Borges y la nada* (London: Tamesis, 1971). Pin-points important aspects of Borges' thought with emphasis on his inner malaise.

11a. Friedman, Mary Lusky, *The Emperor's Kites* (Durham, NC: Duke U.P., 1987). Contains insightful comments and postulates a unifying pattern in Borges' tales.

11b. Lindstrom, Naomi, *Jorge Luis Borges: A Study of the Short Fiction* (Boston: Twayne, 1990). Expository and descriptive. Mainly for the general reader.

12. Milleret, Jean de, *Entretiens avec Jorge Luis Borges*, (Paris: Pierre Bollond, 1967). Further useful declarations by Borges.

13. Murillo, Luis A., *The Cyclical Night: Irony in James Joyce and Jorge Luis Borges* (Cambridge, MA: Harvard U.P., 1968). Full of strange jargon, but useful on 'El jardín de senderos que se bifurcan' and 'La muerte y la brújula'.

14. Pérez, Alberto C., *Realidad y suprarrealidad en los cuentos fantásticos de Jorge Luis Borges* (Miami: Universal, 1971). The critical work most directly concerned with *Ficciones*.

14a. Shaw, Donald L., *Borges' Narrative Strategies* (Liverpool: Francis Cairns, 1992). Deals primarily with Borges' fictional techniques.

14b. Sturrock, John, *Paper Tigers* (Oxford: Clarendon Press, 1977). Argues that Borges' stories are really about writing.

15. Wheelock, Carter, *The Mythmaker* (Austin: Texas U.P., 1969). To be read with caution. Contains some unlikely interpretations.

## ARTICLES

16. Aguirre, José Maria, 'La solución a una adivinanza propuesta por Jorge Luis Borges', *Bulletin of Hispanic Studies*, 42 (1965), 174-81. On the existential relevance of Borges' stories.

17. Bagby, Albert I., 'The Concept of Time in Jorge Luis Borges', *Romance Notes*, 6 (1964-65), 99-105. Useful, especially for 'El milagro secreto'.

17a. Barrenechea, Ana María, 'Borges y la narración que se autoanaliza', *Nueva Revista de Filología Hispánica*, 24 (1975), 517-27. On his attitude to his tales and how he constructs their symbolic meaning.

18. Bickel, Gisèle, 'La alegoría del pensamiento', *Modern Language Notes*, 88 (1973), 295-316. Very good on Borges' view of the inability of language to express reality, and on the duality in his work.

19. Botsford, Keith, 'About Borges and not about Borges', *Kenyon Review*, 26 (1964), 723-37. More useful statements by Borges.

20. Dauster, Frank, 'Notes on Borges' Labyrinths', *Hispanic Review*, 30 (1962), 142-48. On labyrinths in *El Aleph*: indispensable on this vital topic. See also Luis A. Murillo, 'The Labyrinths of Jorge Luis Borges', *Modern Language Quarterly*, 20 (1959), 259-61, also on *El Aleph*.

20a. Natella, Arthur A., 'Symbolic Colors in the Stories of Jorge Luis Borges', *Journal of Spanish Studies: Twentieth Century*, 2 (1974), 39-48. Interesting on this important aspect of symbolism.

21. Rodríguez Monegal, Emir, 'Symbols in the Work of Borges', in *28* below (325-40), in his disappointing *Borges par lui-même* (Paris: Seuil, 1970), pp.87-113, and in *El cuento hispanoamericano ante la crítica*, ed. Enrique Pupo-Walker (Madrid: Castalia, 1973), pp.92-109. A handy general introduction to some of Borges' major symbols.

22. Sábato, Ernesto, 'Sobre los dos Borges', in 25 below (168-78) and in his *Tres aproximaciones a la literatura de nuestro tiempo* (Santiago de Chile: Universitaria, 1968), pp.31-62. A most important short attack on Borges' work by a distinguished fellow Argentine writer.

23. Scari, Robert M., 'Caracterización y desenlace en los relatos realísticos de Borges', *Symposium*, 26 (1972), 261-70. Helpful for 'El Sur'.

24. Weber, Frances, 'Borges' Stories: Fiction or Philosophy'. *Hispanic Review*, 36 (1968), 124-41. Closely argued. Especially useful for Tlön, Uqbar, Orbis Tertius', 'La lotería en Babilonia', and 'El jardín de senderos que se bifurcan'.

## COLLECTIONS OF ESSAYS ON BORGES

Many have been published, especially just after his death. Among the standard ones are:

25. *Cahiers l'Herne*, 4 (Paris: L'Herne, 1964). Very uneven but with useful contributions by Sábato, Irby, Ibarra, and others.

26. Dunham, Lowell and Ivar Ivask (eds), *The Cardinal Points of Borges* (Norman: Oklahoma U.P., 1972). Orginally *Books Abroad* 45 (1971). Contains excellent essays by Yates, Christ, and Irby, and a handy bibliography.

27. *Iberoromania*, n.s. 3 (1975). Contains important articles by J.B. Hall and Alazraki.

27a. *Jorge Luis Borges*, ed. Jaime Alazraki (Madrid: Taurus, 1976). Not much on *Ficciones*, but a good deal on the reception of Borges internationally and some essays by major critics.

27b. *Jorge Luis Borges*, ed. Harold Bloom (New York: Chelsea House, 1986). Mostly trendy essays, but includes useful remarks on 'La muerte y la brújula', 'El jardín de senderos que se bifurcan', and 'Tlön, Uqbar, Orbis Tertius'.

28. *Modern Fiction Studies*, 19 (1973). Carries thirteen articles (especially interesting are those by T.E. Lyon, Wheelock, and D.W. Foster) and a useful supplement to the bibliography in *30* above.

28a. *Revista Iberamericana*, nos 100-01 (1977). The most inclusive collection so far, with important articles both general and on individual tales, including 'Pierre Menard, autor del Quijote', 'El jardín de senderos que se bifurcan', and 'Tlön, Uqbar, Orbis Tertius'.

29. *Tri-Quarterly*, no.25 (1972). Reprinted as *Prose for Borges* (Evanston: Northwestern U.P., 1974). Again very uneven. Useful for *Ficciones* are the articles by Christ and Alazraki and an interview with Borges.

USEFUL ARTICLES ON INDIVIDUAL STORIES OR GROUPS OF
STORIES IN 'FICCIONES' INCLUDE:

On *Tlön, Uqbar, Orbis Tertius*:
30. Alazraki, Jaime, 'Tlön y Asterión: anverso y reverso de una
    epistemología', *Nueva Narrativa Hispanoamericana*, 1, no.2 (1971),
    21-33. Also in *27a*, above, pp.183-200.
31. Irby, James E., 'Borges and the Idea of Utopia', in *26* above, pp.35-45.
32. Mills, Robert S., 'The theme of Scepticism in Borges' "Tlön, Uqbar,
    Orbis Tertius"', in *Studies in Modern Spanish Literature and Art
    Presented to Helen F. Grant*, ed. Nigel Glendinning (London: Tamesis,
    1972), pp.127-38.

On *El acercamiento a Almostásim*:
33. D'Lugo, Marvin, 'Binary Vision in Borgian Narrative', *Romance Notes*,
    13 (1971-72), 425-31.
33a. Holloway, James E., 'Anatomy of "El acercamiento a Almotásim"',
    *Revista Canadiense de Estudios Hispánicos*, 5 (1980-81), 37-59.

On *Pierre Menard, autor del Quijote:*
34. Newton de Molina, David, 'Sceptical Literary Historicism: A Fictional
    Analogue in Jorge Luis Borges', *Essays in Criticism*, 21 (1971), 57-73.

On *La Biblioteca de Babel*:
35. Perera San Martín, Nicasio, 'La n$^{\text{ième}}$ lecture de "La Biblioteca de
    Babel" de Jorge Luis Borges', *Caravelle*, no.21 (1973), 31-41.

On *El jardín de senderos que se bifurcan*:
36. Himelblau, Jack, 'El arte de Jorge Luis Borges visto en "El jardín de
    senderos que se bifurcan"', *Revista Hispánica Moderna*, 32 (1966), 37-
    42.
36a. Millington, Mark I., 'The Importance of Being Albert',
    *Iberoamerikanisches Archiv*, 14 (1988), 173-86.

On *La forma de la espada*:
36b. McGrady, Donald, 'Prefiguration, Narrative Transgression and Eternal
    Return in Borges's "La forma de la espada"', *Revista Canadiense de
    Estudios Hispánicos,* 12 (1987-88), 141-49.

On *Tema del traidor y del héroe*:
37. Scholes, Robert M., 'A Commentary on "The Theme of the Traitor and
    the Hero"', in his *Elements of Fiction* (New York: Oxford U.P., 1968),
    pp.78-88.

On *La muerte y la brújula*:

*37a*. Fama, Antonio, 'Análisis de "La muerte y la brújula" de Jorge Luis Borges', *Bulletin Hispanique*, 85 (1983), 161-73.

*38*. Gallagher, David P., 'Jorge Luis Borges', in his *Modern Latin American Literature* (London: Oxford U.P., 1973), pp.94-121.

*38a*. Irwin, John T., 'Mysteries we Re-Read', *Modern Language Notes*, 101 (1986), 1168-1215.

*39*. Middleman, L.A., 'Borges, Milton and the Name of the Game', *Modern Language Notes*, 87 (1972), 967-70.

*39a*. Solotorevsky, Myrna, 'La muerte y la brújula', *Neophilologus*, 70 (1986), 547-54.

On *El Sur*:

*40*. Gertel, Zunilda, '"El Sur" de Borges: búsqueda de la identidad en el laberinto', *Nueva Narrativa Hispanoamericana*, 1, no.2 (1971), 35-55.

*41*. Phillips, Allen W., '"El Sur" de Borges', *Revista Hispánica Moderna*, 29 (1963), 140-47. Also in his *Estudios y notas sobre literatura hispanoamericana* (Mexico City: Cultura, 1965), pp.165-75.

*42*. Hall, J. B., 'Borges' "El Sur": A "Jardín de senderos que se bifurcan"?', in 27 above, pp.71-77.

On *La lotería en Babilonia, La biblioteca de Babel, Tlön, Uqbar, Orbis Tertius*, and *El jardín de senderos que se bifurcan*:

*43*. Isaacs, Neil D., 'The Labyrinth of Art in Four *Ficciones* of Jorge Luis Borges', *Studies in Short Fiction*, 6 (1969), 383-94.

# CRITICAL GUIDES TO SPANISH TEXTS

*Edited by*
J.E. Varey, A.D. Deyermond and C. Davies

# CRITICAL GUIDES TO SPANISH TEXTS

*Edited by*
J.E. Varey, A.D. Deyermond and C. Davies